"I had always watched Hattie Kauffman on television and admired her work. She's determined, focused, and a gifted reporter and storyteller. Now I know where she gets it from. Hattie's story of how she 'made it' is the quintessential American success story, only Hattie's childhood was so impoverished she couldn't afford the bootstraps to pull herself up with. I read, stunned by the challenges she has faced, impressed with her ability to overcome them, and grateful for the lessons she has shared. I think you will be too."

—**Deborah Norville**, anchor of *Inside Edition*
and *New York Times* bestselling author

"Hattie Kaufman has a gift. She has always known how to get to the heart of every story. Now she shares what's in her own heart. And that's the best story yet."

—**Harry Smith**, veteran television journalist, CBS/NBC

"*Falling into Place* is a compelling story of life—every dimension of life—well told. From agony to deliverance, from a shattered heart to faith, Hattie's story will resonate at some level with everyone. Read this book. It will nourish your soul."

—**Larry W. Poland, PhD,** chairman and CEO
of Mastermedia International

"In the gripping story of her painful divorce and Christian conversion, TV correspondent Hattie Kauffman teaches us that the seeds of God's love grow strongly oftentimes in the soil of suffering and always in the sunshine of surrender. Whatever cliff you are on, whatever abyss you are facing, *Falling into Place* will fill you with hope for a better tomorrow."

—**Michael Guillen, PhD**, former Harvard physics instructor and
science editor of *ABC News*;
bestselling author of *Can a Smart Person Believe in God?*

"An uplifting, encouraging autobiography."

—PowWow.com

"One of the most emotional books I have ever read."

—*Native Hoop Magazine*

"Stunning... a love song... beautifully written."

—*Digital Journal*

"Hattie doesn't hold back."

—Deborah Mitchell Media Associates

"A beautifully written, stirring work."

—Frequency FM

"A gripping memoir... both interesting and eye opening."

—*Games Fiends*

"... has readers glued to the book from the first page to the last."

—Inland 360

"A must-read book!"

—KENR Radio

"Reminiscent of *The Glass Castle*..."

—*Publishers Weekly*

"A raw narrative... laced with memorable characters."

—*Indian Country Today*

"A remarkable story of perseverance."

—KING TV

"Hattie Kauffman *knows* the power of words."

—*Minneapolis Star and Tribune*

"Marvelous memoir... vivid and unforgettable."

—*Consciousness Magazine*

"Take the time to read Hattie's insightful, deeply moving story."

—Youth With A Mission

"One of the best memoirs to be published in recent years."

—*The News Gazette*

"A very candid and vulnerable memoir."

—Calling All Warriors

# A MEMOIR OF
## *Overcoming*

# Hattie Kauffman

**BakerBooks**

*a division of Baker Publishing Group*
Grand Rapids, Michigan

© 2013 by Hattie Kauffman

Published by Baker Books
a division of Baker Publishing Group
P.O. Box 6287, Grand Rapids, MI 49516-6287
www.bakerbooks.com

Paperback edition published 2014
ISBN 978-0-8010-1705-6

Printed in the United States of America

The Library of Congress has cataloged the hardcover edition as follows:
Kauffman, Hattie.
    Falling into place : a memoir of overcoming / Hattie Kauffman.
      pages cm
    ISBN 978-0-8010-1538-0 (cloth)
      1. Kauffman, Hattie. 2. Christian biography. 3. Television journalists—United States—Biography. 4. Women journalists—United States—Biography.
I. Title.
BR1725.K343A3 2013
277.3'083092—dc23                                 2013009366
[B]

Unless otherwise indicated, Scripture quotations are from the Holy Bible, New International Version®. NIV®. Copyright © 1973, 1978, 1984 by Biblica, Inc.™ Used by permission of Zondervan. All rights reserved worldwide. www.zondervan.com

Scripture quotations labeled CEV are from the Contemporary English Version © 1991, 1992, 1995 by American Bible Society. Used by permission.

Scripture quotations labeled NKJV are from the New King James Version. Copyright © 1982 by Thomas Nelson, Inc. Used by permission. All rights reserved.

Scripture quotations labeled TLB are from *The Living Bible*, copyright © 1971. Used by permission of Tyndale House Publishers, Inc., Wheaton, Illinois 60189. All rights reserved.

Scripture quotations labeled KJV are from the King James Version of the Bible.

All dates, place names, titles, and events in this account are factual. The names of certain characters and some details have been changed in order to protect the privacy of those involved.

The author is represented by Ambassador Literary Agency, Nashville, Tennessee.

17  18  19  20      7  6  5  4

To the descendants of John and Josephine

# Acknowledgments

Thank you, Doris, Jaki, Christine, James, and Tracy for your prayers.

Great gratitude to you, Trisha, for your steadfast guidance and friendship.

To Rick, much love.

To my sisters, Lilly, Jo Ann, Carla, Carlotta, and Claudia, thank you for allowing me to pull back the curtain, just a bit.

Love to those who have walked on: Mom, Dad, brother John . . . and of course, Aunt Teddy.

Chapter 1

The woman in front of me was in no shape to be on television. Her face was lifeless—her eyes red, swollen, vacant. She met my gaze as if begging to be told what to do, but I had no idea how to help her and felt every bit as lost as she looked. All I could think to do was recite the facts as I knew them. Maybe facts would bring clarity and direction.

*You have a shoot this morning. You should take a shower.*

My words bounced off her cold image in the mirror. She wasn't listening.

I turned away, but movement felt nearly impossible under the weight of limbs too heavy to lift. My mind felt as though it were slipping in and out of time and I struggled to stay focused on what I was doing. Thirty minutes passed, maybe an hour. I hardly remembered showering, couldn't recall picking out my outfit or applying my camera-ready makeup. Then I was in the middle of the kitchen, staring at everything and nothing in particular—the kitchen belonged to the woman I was yesterday. This morning, the space didn't seem to know me. The instincts born of habit felt foreign and irrelevant.

*You should eat breakfast.*

But how could I, knowing he was just down the hall?

I tiptoed back past the guest room where he was sleeping and made my way to the master bedroom. Our new bedding looked regal in its gold and burgundy. It was only weeks ago we'd walked around Bloomingdale's and decided which fabric and pattern we liked. The big sleigh bed itself was also new.

*We have a brand-new bed.*

Our wedding photo sat upon the dresser. We looked impossibly young. The groom didn't have a single grey hair. I touched the picture, tracing my fingers over our faces, landing finally on our wedding kiss. We had awakened to this photo for seventeen years.

I carried the picture, in its marble frame, back to the kitchen and set it on the counter to face him when he got up. Then I walked out of the house to begin a three-hour drive to Lompoc for my shoot.

I was in no state to be behind the wheel of a car. As I headed up Sunset Boulevard and got onto the 405 Freeway, I was struggling to see through tears. By the time I merged onto Highway 101, crying became weeping. As I passed Ventura, my weeping turned to wailing. Tissues littered the front seat. Whatever had held me together was gone.

By Santa Barbara, I was cried out. I glanced at the clock, in a brief lucid moment, and realized I was an hour ahead of schedule. It hadn't occurred to me to check the time when I was still at the house. I had simply needed to *go*. I pulled off the highway to regroup, gather myself, and reapply my eye makeup. *Maybe I should try again to eat.*

A few minutes later I found myself being seated in the hushed, elegant breakfast garden of the Four Seasons Hotel, overlooking the ocean. A waiter set freshly squeezed orange juice before me and asked if I'd like a *New York Times.*

*What?*

I stared at him as if he were speaking a foreign language. And then I was angry at his insensitivity. Who reads the *New York Times* on a day like this? Did I *look* like I wanted to read a paper?

*Right. I'm a news correspondent. I read the* New York Times *every day.*

I dumbly shook my head. Not this day.

Gazing at the brilliant blue of the ocean, I didn't notice when food was set before me. When the waiter brought the check, I saw an hour had passed and I'd barely touched my plate. I couldn't recall having a single thought during that time. It was as if I'd been clubbed on the head, so stunned that my thoughts had vanished.

*Am I falling apart? You can't fall apart, Hattie. You never fall apart.*

That thin reassurance sent my mind tumbling back in time, searching for proof of this assertion.


## Look Directly into the Camera

"Focus," I tell myself, facing the huge studio camera.

I am twenty-six years old and about to anchor my first news broadcast. And in Seattle, of all places—the same city that couldn't break us but came close, the city that was supposed to be a new beginning for Mom and Dad when they left the reservation—but where we seven kids found ourselves, more than once, huddled in a parked car on First Avenue waiting for them to come out of a tavern.

"Mom, can we go now? Please?"

"Soon," she'd call to us, before disappearing again into the dark doorway of a bar, while we waited in the cold car. She'd emerge some time later, with a pronouncement of, "Soonly."

"Mom, let's go. We want to go home."

"Soonly," she'd sing. "Soonly."

I pull my mind back from thoughts of my family and our history as I shuffle through the script pages and prepare to report Seattle's morning headlines. Yet, who could've predicted that that shivering, skinny, Indian kid would someday be anchoring the news? Does it show? Will they see how far in over my head I am?

The station's theme music comes on. With the floor director's fingers punching the air just below the camera lens, the countdown begins: five-four-three-two-one—and I'm on . . . live television. Before I'm halfway through reading the second story on the teleprompter, the director's voice crackles through my earpiece, "Drop page six."

My brain works two paths. I am reading, hitting the words with overemphasized inflection, as I try to give them meaning and weight, while simultaneously reaching down to pull page six out of the pile in front of me and sliding it to the side. The teleprompter rolls on.

This chance to anchor is a complete fluke. I'm the rookie in the newsroom, a reporter for only a year. But the early morning newscast has just one anchor and one overnight reporter, and last night they both called in sick.

When my phone rang in the middle of the night, the managing editor asked if I knew how to anchor.

"Of course," I said, although I had never read from a teleprompter and had zero experience.

There's no makeup person in local morning news, so I apply my own powder and lipstick. Too much? Not enough? My long brown hair hangs down my back. I look like what I am, a recent grad student and newly divorced mom of two kids who are depending on me to make it as a news reporter.

*They're probably just waking up now to get ready for school.*

*Now's not the time to think about that. Focus, Hattie. We're going to a commercial break. Look directly into the camera. Smile.*

"No, you didn't fall apart," I whispered, as if it was the me of twenty-five years ago that needed a pat on the back. *You bluffed your way onto the air and became an anchorwoman, and then a network correspondent, and now . . .* I glanced about the luxurious restaurant like I'd just been dropped into the present, noticing the check the waiter had left on the table, a big bill for uneaten food, and remembered that even now a camera crew was waiting for me.

I paid the breakfast bill and continued north on Highway 101. By the time I arrived at the shoot in Lompoc, I appeared so ravaged the producer averted her eyes and inhaled, as if buying time to figure out how to tell me I looked like roadkill.

Our assignment was a feature story on a thriving home business that sold products from Africa. I interviewed the owner, a billowy black woman, who told me God had awakened her one morning with the distinct message that she must help women in Africa.

I gave a routine, disconnected nod—partly in an attempt to mask my annoyance at being dragged all the way up here to talk to a crazy woman who seriously believed God had spoken to her, and partly because no matter what she was saying, I simply could not bring myself to fully engage with her. Her responses sounded like static in my ears. I hardly asked a single follow-up question to anything she said. So she kept speaking and I kept nodding. But as we went on, her dark eyes bored into mine.

"God woke me up," she repeated.

## The Long Road

"Wake up. Hattie, wake up."

I am seven years old and my little sister Carla is shaking me awake. Blinking against the brightness of the lightbulb overhead, I give her a cranky face, roll over, and close my eyes again.

"Wake up. We're going to Idaho," she urges.

I sit up. It is the middle of the night. Every light in the house is on. Bleary eyed, I see Carla has a paper bag in her hand and is looking for clothes to throw into it, while the youngest two girls are still asleep at my feet. The scene doesn't make sense to my drowsy brain.

"Come on, girls." Mom's yell comes from the bottom of the stairs, in the high, nasally pitch that lets me know I'd better jump. It's another After Closing Time Road Trip.

We never know when one might happen. A year could go by, or we might have two in one month. It could be in the summer or during the school year. We groggily pile into the backseat of the car. She throws a blanket over us and we speed off into the night. Somewhere in the desert, sunrise will jerk us awake. Mom might have pulled over and be asleep, or she might be squinting hard against the light, still driving, a beer bottle between her knees.

I can't guess what Idaho is for her.

For me, it's a ton of tough cousins, girls who hit like boys, some who make fun of us for being half white. But it also means Grandma and the smell of pies baking. And cold rivers, tall pine trees, Grandpa's gentle laugh, and . . .

"Hey, wake up." My sister shakes me again. "We're in Idaho. We're here."

## A Thousand Miles Away

I shook off the memory, returning my attention to the African American woman, who hopefully had no idea my thoughts were in another time and place. She seemed to be waiting for me to respond and so I nodded, feigning understanding, while inwardly wondering at my sudden inability to remain in the here and now.

"I could not ignore God," she continued, leaning forward and staring at me until my own discomfort made me look down at my notes. After a pause she went on, "Even though I had no idea how to proceed, I couldn't ignore him."

The certainty of her words reached into my fog and pulled at me. For the first time, I felt myself leaning forward. Something here felt true and personal. *Does she see? Does she know?* I pushed my intrigue aside and settled back in my chair again, hurrying through the rest of the interview and just wanting it to be over.

As the crew was breaking down the gear and I was gathering my things to leave, the woman approached me. She grabbed hold of my arms and looked at me again with those dark eyes. "Women all over the world will be praying for you," she said.

*Praying for me?*

And then, this extraordinary person embraced me, full-on hugged me. Despite my astonishment, part of me wanted to press into her and collapse into those sheltering arms. But I stiffened and pulled back. *Why bother*, I thought. *It's too late.* I didn't need her pity. Or her God.

## Walk Away Hollow

"I don't want the white man's God," I whisper harshly into the phone, turning my back so my sisters and brother won't hear me. We are gathered around the phone in the living room, which we do whenever Aunt Teddy calls.

"Oh, Hattie," Teddy begins, her voice thin and tinny over the long-distance line.

It is 1970. I am fifteen and disgusted that I was ever taken in by her words. No loving God could have created my world.

"It's not a white man's God, Hattie. Christ died for *all* people."

"The missionaries just wanted to steal our land," I sneer. "The government needed to tame the Indians, so they sent in the Christians."

"But—"

"I don't want to hear anymore. I'm finished with it."

I drop the receiver dismissively into the hand of the next sister in line waiting to talk to Aunt Teddy. In rejecting her God, I am pushing away the only person who has consistently been kind to me. I walk away hollow.

## Unsteady Steps

I practically staggered back to my car, so desperate was I to get away from the camera crew and the intense lady talking about God. It's a wonder I didn't kill anyone that day, driving six hours on freeways, in and out of tears, in and out of focus. Just as I was reaching the outer edge of Los Angeles, my cell phone rang.

"Hi, it's me," he said.

*"It's me?" Does he think I've already forgotten his voice?*

"Hi," I answered, tempted to add, "It's me."

"Do you want to get dinner?" he asked.

*He's back.*

"Yes!" I exclaimed. "Do you want to go out? Or shall we eat at home?"

"At home," he said, and added, "I love you."

I relaxed into my seat, exhausted. We'd have dinner and let go of last night's madness.

The kitchen was mine again as I prepared lamb shank, sure that he was on his way home to give me an explanation.

Later, as I set the table, I heard the door handle click. In expectation, I swung around to meet him, only to feel my smile falter at the sight of his stilted posture.

He came through the door but couldn't quite enter the room. My movements slowed as I placed the food on the table. He set down his briefcase.

"Hi," he said.

"Hi."

"Smells good," he offered.

"I made lamb shank."

He could see that.

"I thought lamb shank would be good."

There was no reason to keep repeating it, but I frantically grabbed it like a life raft.

"You always liked lamb shank."

16

"It smells good," he repeated, walking like a stick figure to take his seat at the table. Unwilling to give up the ritual, I put salt and pepper before him, and took my seat as well. In silence, we picked up our knives and forks. The enormous quiet pressed against me, forcing my mind to scramble for something to say, as if a pleasantry like, "How was your day?" might save the situation. But before I could begin, he blurted, "I want to be perfectly clear. I want a divorce."

"Divorce?"

He seemed surprised at my surprise.

"What did you think I meant last night?"

"Well . . ."

*Of course, he had meant divorce.*

"But you didn't use the D-word," I said lamely.

"I didn't?"

"No. You didn't."

We set down our utensils. No one cared about lamb shank.

"I didn't say the word 'divorce'?" he asked, incredulously.

He shook his head and muttered to himself, ". . . and I've really been trying to work on my honesty."

Something about the introspective expression on his face made me conscious of the vast expanse between us; me, merely a bystander witnessing a man wonder at his own lack of honesty. Then, as if he remembered I was in the room, he turned to me with a whip of his head and declared, "Yes. I want a divorce." He said it with the inflection of someone deciding which salad dressing to order in a restaurant. "Yes, I'll have the bleu cheese. Yes, I want a divorce."

"But . . . but . . . how come?" I felt as though I was stumbling over my own feet. "Is there someone else?"

"It's not about that," he dismissed.

"Well, what is it about?"

He retreated into something from the previous night's refrain: "I have to live according to my commitments."

I had no idea what that meant the first time he said it and the repetition of it now seemed robotic—rehearsed, even.

"But our marriage *is* our commitment."

"Our marriage is a fraud," he answered.

*Since when?*

"I have to live in integrity," he said, through gritted teeth.

*What does that mean?*

A wallop of fear wouldn't allow me to ask if integrity meant being true to someone else, if there were another commitment that I was not aware of. Nothing in me felt brave enough to hear the answer, and so, as if covering up the topic, I placed my hand over his.

"Why, honey? Why divorce? I don't understand."

When he didn't answer, I continued asking, a third and fourth time. He met these questions by darting his eyes about, to his plate, to the ceiling, out the window. At last, in a rushing exhale, he blurted, "You're just not suitable at business dinners."

*What?*

"You just, you make everyone uncomfortable," he added. "You're socially awkward. All my friends say I'm more myself when you're not around."

Disbelief turned to a tortured attempt to entertain his premise and argue against it. I reminded him of the couple who'd been trying for weeks to get together with us for dinner. They certainly didn't seem to be uncomfortable with me. In fact, the wife and I had talked on the phone the other day about scheduling dinner. I recalled suddenly that we'd set the date for next week.

*We can't get a divorce. We're having dinner with friends.*

"Forget it, I already told them." He shrugged.

My hand shot up to cover my mouth. Had she known when we were on the phone? Humiliation hit me. To avoid absorbing it, I clawed my way back to his suggestion that I make people uncomfortable and, ridiculously, did a mental scan of all the other couples we'd dined with recently, and mentioned one.

"They were *very* uncomfortable at dinner," he replied.

"You're divorcing me because your friends were uncomfortable at dinner?"

"No," he sighed. "That's not it. It's . . ."

"What?" I repeated. "What is it?"

Shifting in his seat, his visible distress jolted me with a new possibility.

*He's dying and he doesn't want to tell me.*

That would explain the determined coldness, the hurtful words. He was shutting off debate . . . to protect me from having to go through his death. Like a contortionist, I twisted my thinking so that betrayal could appear as kindness. I invented one diagnosis after another, from a brain tumor to Alzheimer's.

"Are you sick? Is that it?" I asked, caressing his shoulder.

"No," he said, looking down at the table as if speaking to the cold, congealing lamb shank.

"Then, why? Just tell me, why?"

In the silence of his non-answers, my mind raced. An image of the trendy pair of jeans I'd noticed a few weeks ago came to mind. It wasn't just the tight jeans. Everything right down to his underwear was brand-new. In fact, his wardrobe had undergone such a strange overhaul that perhaps . . .

"Are you gay?" I asked.

"No!" he blared, finally turning toward me, indignant. "What makes you think that?"

"I'm just trying to understand," I answered. "Why would you want to end our marriage? We're not fighting. We don't have problems. I just don't understand."

Facing me directly, he declared in a flat, staccato voice, punctuating each word, "I don't enjoy being with you."

It was such a slap that even my gasp caught in my throat.

Our eyes held each other for a beat before mine dropped; my gaze settled upon my long-married hands limp in my lap. Desperate for distraction, my brain burrowed in on minute details. I noticed veins visible underneath tan and crackled skin. They were Mom's hands.

"Well . . ." I heard my ghost voice say.

He continued, "I just *settled* for you because I was tired of being alone, and you were pretty then."

*I was pretty then.*

"Well . . ." I echoed myself.

My eyes wandered from my hands to his. I saw his knuckles were white, and that his right fist clenched something. It was the steak knife.

"Perhaps we should remove the knives from the table?" I suggested, with as much lightness as I could summon, which made it come out like an ill-timed joke.

He dropped the knife with a clatter.

Though my body balked, I willed my muscles to move, to pick up the utensils and dishes of uneaten food and carry them to the kitchen.

"Stick the knives in my back," he choked out. "I deserve it."

He began to sob.

The most I could manage was to swivel halfway around to witness his narrow shoulders heave, see his head drop to his chest, and listen to him weep. I was too stupefied to question whether his crying was for me, whether it held any compassion or shame for what he had just said or what he had just done.

The old me would have rushed to soothe him. The newly discarded me turned vacantly to the domestic duties of cleaning up after supper. Perhaps another woman would have stalked out the door, or grabbed his bright new wardrobe and thrown it on the lawn. A therapist once told me that adult children of alcoholics are often irrationally loyal. I don't know if that was the case, but washing dirty dishes seemed the only thing to do, and so there I was, rinsing silverware, loading the dishwasher, scraping plates into the garbage, throwing away perfectly good food.

## Famished

"This child is undernourished," Teacher says, as she hands me over to the school nurse. "Just look how thin she is."

They huddle in quiet talk.

I peek about the exam room, excited to be somewhere new. A box of tongue depressors attracts me, the wood smooth and splinter free. I want to spill them onto the counter and build something. Just as I go up on my tiptoes to reach for them, the nurse grips my shoulder and turns me toward her.

She lifts my shirt and runs her finger over each rib, like a stick slapping against the slats of a fence. I decide she must be counting my ribs. Teacher, watching us, shakes her head, as if she's saying no. I think that means the nurse is counting wrong. There's an upside-down U in my chest where the ribs meet in the middle. The nurse hooks her finger under it, like she's going to lift me. She frowns and shakes her head just like Teacher.

I am a kindergartener.

We live in the housing projects. And usually, we are hungry. At home one day my sister eats Tide soap. It's in a bowl, on a shelf, looking like sugar. She swallows it before she tastes it.

One afternoon Mom comes home, which alone is a big event. But this time it's tremendous. She has bags of groceries. We swarm her, all seven kids jumping, talking, laughing, trying to hug her and grab something to eat at the same time. I snatch a loaf of bread and run upstairs to hide it in a closet.

Later, when Mom finishes putting away the canned vegetables, milk, and butter, she notices the bread is missing.

"For Pete's sake, did the clerk not put it in the bag?"

I don't say a word. I sit on the couch, staring at my curled up toes. Food is more crucial than honesty. I am learning that my survival is up to me.

# Chapter 2

I hungered for an answer, but couldn't find one. A divorce out of the blue didn't make sense. Pacing my room, I wondered if it could be my fault. Stopping mid-stride, I asked myself what in *me* could have led to this? With the thought, I dropped my head to take in my body. Oh yeah, the breast cancer. But the surgery, radiation, and reconstruction took place years ago. It couldn't be that. Yet . . . maybe I'd become too nagging. I'd had a hysterectomy, because of the cancer risk, and surgical menopause can make women irritable. It said so right there in the pamphlet at the doctor's office. I must have gotten so outrageously irritable that I'd irritated myself out of my marriage.

I walked to the mirror to seek clues in my reflection. *You were pretty then.* Was it a lack of prettiness? My reflection showed weariness, but my face was not so horrible that I should be discarded like some old sock.

Flopping onto my bed, I closed my eyes against the obvious. It wasn't that my looks were gone, it was that my eyes and ears were gone. I'd become deaf and blind to the affair that he must have been having. There had to have been warning signs and I had missed them. I was the clichéd middle-aged woman, astonished to find herself . . .

*Dumped. I'm being dumped.*

It was too much. On top of the rejection, I felt the appalling reality that this would be my *second* divorce. I'd be a twice-divorced woman. It didn't matter that the first had been a teenage marriage . . . two stupid kids acting out their parents' drinking and fighting.

Now it was happening again, only without the alcohol and drama. And bafflingly, this was supposed to be the grown-up marriage, the one that wasn't a reenactment of craziness. Yet, there it was: a different sort of insane, one tediously common. Older guy dumps long-term wife. Feeling so sick I couldn't sit still, I hopped off the bed to pace.

*This happens to other people. I've done stories about them. I've interviewed those women. But I'm not supposed to be one of them.*

Tinier than a tremble, a slight shaking began in my center and grew until I rattled all the way out to my fingertips. I was being thrown away. There had to be a mistake. Crumpling, I crossed my arms over my belly, unconsciously bending in on myself. We were buying a condo in Hawaii. We were planning our retirements. We . . .

*Could it really be that I'm not enjoyable to be around?* I popped up straight again and considered the accusation: socially awkward.

I sat down once again upon the bed. *Being married to me must be awful.* As a network correspondent, I was often on the road and could be called away on a moment's notice. I had a suitcase packed at all times, sitting there in the garage ready to toss into a taxi, and another one in my office. My passport was in my purse next to my cell phone, which could ring at any time with instructions to head to the airport. Maybe he couldn't take being married to someone who always had a foot out the door, and "home" was the place I visited.

Poking further into that corner, I recalled the times, years ago, when he'd said, "I feel like I'm last on your list. After your job, after your kids, after your cabin, after your sisters, you finally consider me." Yes, he had said that—more than once. I remembered telling people at work, producers and other correspondents, wondering whether their spouses made similar complaints.

*It's because I'm gone all the time on work assignments.*

I fell back on the bed, lying sideways across it, thinking. *No, that couldn't be it. I was a correspondent before we got married.* Why would a spouse accommodate a career for almost two decades, and then suddenly decide it's the reason to leave? It wasn't the hours I kept, it was something else.

I stared up at the ceiling, examining it as if an explanation were hidden in it. The bland, creamy surface revealed nothing. I was left with the cliché, comical in its everydayness: aging man, finally feeling financial success, dumps the old ball and chain.

Still, I couldn't shake the feeling that there had to be something lacking in me. Who else was there to blame? I was guilty of marrying someone who would abandon me, so therefore I must have brought it upon myself.


## My Fault

Drunk people, that's what I know. I wake at night to the roar of Mom, Dad, and the occasional others who stumble in with them. Like my parents, the drinking buddies appear and then vanish. Bursts of laughter careen into foul words as they battle or weep, pass out and wake up mean. One of them cuts off my hair.

Smeared orange lipstick colors her frown.

"Lice," the lips spit at my tangles. "Nits."

Scissors, in unsteady hands, clip back and forth across my head. I don't know who she is.

"There," the bright lips pronounce. "That's better." She drops the scissors and sways out of the mess that is our living room on a morning after.

Some days later—at some point we stop counting—Mom rolls

in. She freezes when she sees me and orders me to come closer. I lower my head in a reflex of shame.

"Who did this?"

My feet dangle in the air as she lifts me to face her.

"Who cut your hair?"

Each word sends a poof of booze smell up my nose as I struggle for an answer to her question, but I don't know the lady's name. She had orange lipstick. She was here with Dad.

In the face of Mom's anger, I cannot find the words to tell her it's not my fault; I didn't ask the lady to cut my hair. She just did it. She did it *to* me. I didn't know I was supposed to stop her. I am so ashamed.

As she begins shaking me, Mom's fingernails cut into my underarms.

*Think*, I tell myself, but no name comes to mind, just the smudged lips mouthing, "Rat's nest of nits."

Mom twirls me around toward my brother and sisters.

"Who cut Hattie's hair?"

With my eyes, I beg my siblings to help but they're too scared to say a word. My choppy locks flip back and forth as Mom tries to shake the truth out of me, bringing only tears from all of us. And then, she's gone.

Dad's presence is equally erratic, equally unnerving. He disappears and reappears, without a pattern. Our parents might be gone for a night, or a week. Sometimes they are together, often they are not. We fend for ourselves.

John is the oldest, with Lilly right behind. They trade off the duties of being the Boss, telling us when to come in from playing, when to eat, when to go to bed. If they leave the house, Annie, the next oldest and just finishing first grade, becomes the Boss.

On this day, it's my turn. I am four years old. John, Lilly, and Annie are outside playing. I'm in charge of the Kids: Carla, Lotta, and Baby. I don't know why only those three are called the Kids, since none of us are grown up.

We're hungry.

There's nothing to eat.

Three-year-old Carla and two-year-old Lotta trail me into the kitchen, where the linoleum is cold under my feet. I carry Baby on my hip. Pots and pans lie scattered across the floor from the drum game we played earlier. Lotta gets distracted by them and starts pounding on a pan, until I open the fridge.

"I wan' some," she says, toddling over to grab my leg.

There's no milk or cheese in the fridge. It's as empty as the last time I checked. The scraped-out mayonnaise jar is still next to a finished but never tossed out jar of pickled pig's feet, Dad's hangover cure. Sighing, I close the door and turn away.

"I'm hungry," Carla complains when we parade back to the living room.

"Hu-gree," Lotta echoes.

One at a time, the Kids fuss, whimper, and build to a cry, like they're taking turns at it. At last, Baby falls asleep on my lap, signaling Carla and Lotta to drift off, slumped against each other on the couch. The resulting silence is so sudden it scares me. Without the Kids to look after, I'm abruptly aware no one is looking after me. I somehow know that this isn't how things should be, that someone should be taking care of me. But who?

The quiet feels like something's about to pounce. With growing panic, I tell myself not to cry. *You're too big to cry. You're almost five. You're the Boss.*

Afraid to look to the left or right, I focus on the front door that will open to John, Lilly, and Annie. I picture them returning with laughter, and teasing, and . . . bags of food.

Hunger.

The growls in my stomach clutch at my attention and scatter

my fear. There has to be something in the kitchen. I slide Baby off my lap to make another search.

I can't reach the cupboards high above the kitchen counter, so I pull out a low drawer, and another one above it, as a makeshift step ladder so I can climb up onto the counter. The first cupboard is empty. The next holds a saltine cracker tin but I know there's nothing in it but old photos of Mom and Dad when they used to be happy. Still, the cracker printed on the outside of the tin makes my mouth water.

I peer across to the far side of the sink where there's one more cupboard. *I can make it*, I tell myself. My tiny feet balance along the narrow edge of the sink to the far counter. There, I open the last cupboard and see a coffee tin, a beer glass on its side, mismatched salt and pepper shakers, some matchbooks Dad is saving, and a little packet of half-burnt birthday candles.

Hopping down to the floor, I return to the fridge and look again at the empty mayonnaise jar, the pickled pig's feet label. I give up and start to close the fridge when I see it: a jam jar on one of the narrow shelves built into the door. Jam! I grab the jar and hold it to my chest to twist off the top. It's empty. But . . . but no—there's a smudge of purple along the bottom rim. I rush for a knife to scrape it into my mouth. As I'm scooping up the bit of jelly, I hear Baby's first whimpers from the living room.

*I don't want to share.*

I swallow the taste of jam, gulping it down as her cries grow louder. Instantly, I feel a new weight: guilt. I have eaten the only food.

Baby wails.

I tilt the empty jar. I scrape what's already been scraped. The knife comes up empty.

Her cries are an accusation. I could have shared some with her. I should have.

Dropping the knife, I stick my fist into the jar and slide my finger along the bottom. When I pull it out, there's a speckle of jam, tinier than a half kernel of corn, on my fingernail. Concentrating on the purple fleck, I walk carefully back to the living room and put my finger in Baby's mouth.

She is soothed, sucking the speck of jam, but it doesn't take away the shameful feeling inside me.

I can't forget it, even when the older ones come in from playing, red-faced and loud. I fear they will see my greediness, but they don't. Instead, they yell at me and the younger kids for the wet spots on the couch, for not changing Baby's diaper, for being "too old to pee in your pants," for crying or whining. They're right, I'm sure. I must deserve their scolding.

John sends us upstairs to the bathroom, while Lilly goes to the kitchen to look for food. After a while, we hear her shout.

"Mush!"

We stampede back down to find her standing on the counter holding a brown bag over her head like a trophy.

"Mush." She beams.

We gather around to look at the odd bag.

"Us-duh." Annie tries sounding out the lettering.

John grabs it, and reads with authority, "USDA surplus commodity oatmeal."

"Mush!" the big ones exclaim together.

Lilly hops down and picks a pan up off the floor.

"Who made this mess?"

I suck in a breath, certain I'm in trouble, but no one really cares about the pots and pans all over the place, because there is mush. In minutes, it is boiling and releasing an aroma that pulls us to the stove. We're like cats meowing around Lilly's feet, until she orders us out.

"Go sit down. Get the kids out of here. It's almost ready."

Our family gathers at the table, empty cups or bowls before

28

us. When Lilly carries the pot to the table, there is an awe even the littlest ones sense. They don't whine or fidget, but gape at the steam rising from the mush.

"We should pray," John says quietly.

We are not a religious family and I have no idea how John knows to pray. Families on television do it. Maybe that's where he got the idea. *No, from Aunt Teddy*, I think, *or from Grandma and Grandpa*. I would like to believe that God will take care of us, but my idea of God is pretty empty. I just copy the bigger kids and do what they do.

We fold our hands before us, and together say, "God is great. God is good. Thank you for this food we eat. Amen."

## Lost Appetite

My husband and I ate together just once more after the "divorce dinner," and only because I haplessly wandered into it one morning. We were in that awkward phase, the "D" word spoken but not acted upon. I was still too stunned to do anything, stumbling about in a mist so thick I couldn't see or feel. Meanwhile, his moods appeared to fluctuate, unnerving me with the unexpected.

"Hi." He smiled when I walked into the kitchen, on my way to work. "Did you see the game?"

It took me a moment to decipher the words.

*Could he really be talking about football?*

I shook my head in silence.

He jumped into a description of passes, tackles, kicks, and punts; a monologue punctuated now and then with the words "Michigan" and "Ohio State."

Maybe it was the mundane normalcy of husband-game-talk that put me on autopilot. I reverted to routine, which meant a bowl of cereal. But the falseness of the situation bore down on me and it took every bit of concentration to do what I'd done a million times. As if detached from my body, I watched my physical movements, saw my hand reach for the cupboard, grasp the bowl, my movements overly precise.

*Open the fridge. Get the milk. Pour the milk.*

He sat at the table, rattling on. I saw he'd put a placemat out for me but I couldn't make myself walk over there to sit with him. Despite the outward appearance of a couple's morning ritual, I knew it wasn't real. I stood at the counter and took a bite of my cereal, making myself nod at his football story, before realizing sports wasn't the topic anymore.

"It's really changed my digestive system," he said, half-turned in his chair to face me. I forced myself to pay attention to his words.

*He's talking about the inner workings of his gut.*

Contemplation of his intestinal health was more than my own stomach could take. Carrying my cereal bowl as though it might disintegrate at any moment, I walked cautiously to the sink and slowly poured its contents down the drain.

"These supplements changed my whole system. If you want to try some, the powder's right there." He gestured toward the counter while looking at me expectantly.

I stifled an urge to laugh, then had to clamp down an impulse to scream. It was my first true inkling of anger. Why had it taken me so long to feel the one emotion I *deserved* to feel? Any anger I'd allowed had been turned toward myself, not him. And even now, the edge of rage dissipated as quickly as it had come, washed over by unexpected pity for the aging man turned in his chair, awaiting my acknowledgment. His was the simplest of requests: one human being who just wanted another to listen to him. Yet I'd been fired from the listening job. In sharp relief I saw the sadness of the moment. We no longer knew how to interact. In a paralysis of not knowing what I was supposed to feel, what I was allowed to feel, I backed away.

"Thanks," I muttered. "I've got to get to work."

"OK." He smiled. As I walked out the door, he called out a compliment, "Nice dress!"

Unsettling, unpredictable, and as yet unavoidable, these sporadic encounters continued. At times you'd think the word *divorce* had never been uttered. Yet one day he handed me a list of realtors with the briskness one might use at the office.

"Choose one, so we can put the house up for sale," he said. "It's the only thing we own together. We'll just sell it, split the money and be done."

He'd already added up our separate assets, he said, and they remarkably came out exactly even, so neither would owe the other anything in the divorce. He presented his tally: a piece of paper with handwritten columns, one with his name at the top, the other with mine. There were the checking accounts, retirement funds, even the dollar value of our two cars. Seventeen years of marriage reduced to scribbles on a page that proved, he said, we didn't need to spend a bunch of money on lawyers. To go our separate ways, all we had to do was sell the house and split the money from the sale.

## Cash Me In

"Money, we need money," John whispers intensely.

He is pressed flat on his belly, peering under the couch. Lilly, on her knees in a pile of clothes on the floor, digs through pockets. So far, they have two pennies and a nickel.

"Help out," Lilly growls at Annie, who stands, stretches, and ambles over to the table to look under the dirty dishes.

"Not there." Lilly sighs. "Get over here and help me lift up the rug."

I sit with the Kids on the couch, unsure what the hunt for money means. Carla hugs her knees. Lotta picks a scab. Baby sucks her thumb, and wiggles her way onto my lap. I'm about to ask how come they're looking for money, when Lilly springs to her feet in a little dance.

"A dime!"

John jumps up to check.

"We're rich," Annie marvels, which makes Lilly elbow her.

John counts the money: one dime, one nickel, and two pennies. John and Lilly look at each other and nod. In their silent language, they've come to a conclusion. Without saying anything to the rest of us, they walk out the front door.

"What's going on?" I ask Annie.

"Baby's first birthday, stupid," she says, squeezing me off the couch, while at the same time lifting Baby from my lap. "Put the dirty dishes in the sink. Get this place ready. We're having a party."

After a while, John and Lilly return, carrying a small paper bag and hustling into the kitchen. I'm excited, pondering how a party could fit in that little bag.

"Close the shades to make it dark," Lilly orders.

Annie pulls a chair to the window, climbs up on it, and reaches above her head for the string that pulls the shade down.

"OK, ready," she calls back.

John and Lilly emerge with flickering light on their faces from a used birthday candle burning in the middle of a Hostess chocolate cupcake.

"Happy birthday dear B-a-a-a B-e-e-e, happy birthday to you," we sing quickly because the stub of candle is almost down to the frosting.

Baby doesn't know she's supposed to blow it out, so we do it for her.

"Since it's her very first birthday," John decrees, "she gets the cupcake all to herself."

"Oh . . ." The rest of us deflate.

"Don't worry," he smiles. "Two came in a pack. We'll split the other one."

Lilly brings the other Hostess chocolate cupcake to the table and, with a butter knife, cuts it precisely in half. Hungrily, we watch the movement of her hand as she divides each half into three more slices. When all six of us have a sliver, we begin, each savoring the taste and texture for as long as we can.

Licking my lips and each one of my fingers, I turn toward Baby, take in her chocolate-smeared chin and feel a bubbling joy. Until I realize that no one told Baby to make a wish. She's too young to know on her own and no one told her. I fret at a lost chance to wish.

# Chapter 3

It was life on the edge from the very beginning. When I was born, our family lived on the outermost boundary of the Nez Perce Indian Reservation, which begins at the confluence of the Snake and Clearwater rivers. In 1955, as my mom went into labor, she and Dad piled their three kids, John, Lilly, and Annie, into the car and drove sixty miles along the twisting Clearwater River to drop them with Grandma and Grandpa. Then they turned up a steep gravel road that scaled a canyon, in a series of switchbacks, from the river valley up to the prairie, another forty miles away. They barely made it through the front door of the hospital in Grangeville, Idaho, before I popped out.

It figures.

My mother, Josephine, was never one for caution. Preferring the names Josie or "Jo Jo," she was petite but strong, or as she used to say, small but mighty. Rather than attend an Indian boarding school, she dared to stay in public school, one of the few brown faces at graduation. Afterward, she threw some clothes into a suitcase and took a chance on life off the reservation. She got a job in Spokane driving a forklift during World War II, and somewhere during those daring days, she met John Kauffman, or Johnnie, a soldier home from the front. A scar snaking across his belly showed he'd already beaten death. He seemed to have nothing to lose. Johnnie and Josie hit it off immediately.

Scoffing at taboos against interracial unions, the full-blooded Nez Perce woman and the soldier who'd been taunted by fellow troops for his German last name married and set about building a family.

Photos, kept in that saltine tin in the cupboard, showed them smiling at one another, happy in the early years. There were snapshots of the first baby, John Jr., swaddled tightly and held between them. Other black and white shots captured him as a dark-haired toddler astride a Shetland pony, Mom at his side. Lilly arrived and was duly photographed, her babyhood to toddler ages chronicled. But something stopped the cameras after that. There would come a time when we later-born would hold these rare photos in our hands with the reverence accorded the sacred. Mom's smile. Dad's confidence. The smartly dressed toddlers lifted in their arms. The images seemed from another world.

Three years after Lilly, Jo Ann was born and they called her Annie. Next up, Mom was ready to have another son; in fact, she was sure she would have a boy and was all set to name him Allan. But after their mad dash up the canyon, there in the lobby of the Grangeville hospital, the doctor lifted her newborn and Mom saw . . . a girl. She didn't bother coming up with a girl name. She stuck an E on the end of Allan, and for a month I was Allane. It was only when her grandmother Hattie died thirty days after my birth that Mom decided that should be my name, but it was never changed on my birth certificate and half the time they called me "Laney," which vaguely reminded me that I was supposed to be Allan.

It wasn't until adulthood that I learned Mom and her older sister had been pregnant at the same time, each hoping for a boy to be named after their only brother, Allan. It was a gestational race for naming rights. Mom, first into labor, must have been smiling through her contractions as the car careened up the canyon to the hospital, certain her willpower would produce a son. That was Mom. One of her favorite sayings was, "Where there's a will, there's a way." Naturally, there was no girl name ready in reserve, hence the E stuck on the end of Allan. (Several weeks later, her sister gave birth to a bruiser of a boy whom she immediately named Allan, but his very size inspired relatives to good-naturedly call him "Pee Wee," a name that stuck his entire life, thus negating the sibling rivalry over a name that in the end wasn't used much by either me or my cousin.)

Mom never got her second boy. By the time her last three children were born, one girl after the other, each only a year apart, she kept the naming simple: Carla, Carlotta, and Claudia. That was too much of a tongue twister for the rest of us, so we called them Carla, Lotta, and Baby, collectively known as the Kids. By then, our family was on its way to fracture, though we didn't know it.

In 1960, Mom and Dad packed us all into a car and moved us to Seattle, in search of jobs and "a better life," I imagine. Who knows the dreams of Johnnie and Josie as they headed west? They must have hoped for the best, perhaps reaching once more for the smiles frozen in the black and white photographs carried along in a tin box. We were moving away from the reservation to build a new home in the city. It must have sounded good. In reality, we were headed for the Projects. None of us imagined it was possible to live on less than nothing. To eat less than nothing.

We kids, jostling in the backseat of the car, had no idea that soon we would spend days or even weeks on our own. Just staying alive would require everything we had.

## Abundance

My husband waved his arm and turned in a semicircle, admiring our richly appointed living room.

"Sometimes I think . . . oh, I don't know . . . maybe we shouldn't get a divorce, because we have all this stuff. I mean . . . we have all . . . this."

After surveying the room, he glanced in my direction.

"In a way, it would be a shame. And you don't nag like the wives of my friends."

I tried tuning him out while flipping through the mail quickly. I'd come to recognize this pattern of his—speaking out loud, but without any recognition that I could be a part of this debate he was having with . . . himself.

After a contemplative pause, he concluded, "No. I'm going to do it."

I was glad I hadn't bothered entering the conversation.

When he walked past me, disappearing down the hall, I looked around at the furniture, at the room full of "stuff." He saw all of these *things* so clearly, but where was I? With my outrage tucked safely away again, I had drifted into the background. Remaining unseen must have felt safer. Even as I told this story to my friend, Jeanie, I was flat. Numb.

"Debating whether to divorce his wife right in front of her?" she exclaimed.

Autumn sun slid through the windows of her Beverly Hills condo. The bright green of her country French décor reflected the light, making it all too brilliant for me. I squinted, feeling exposed.

I hadn't told any of my relatives or co-workers, but to Jeanie, I had just spilled it all.

"You're not *comforting* him, are you?" she asked.

"We've hugged a couple times."

"Those hugs aren't for you," she dismissed. "They're for him! He wants a hug from Mommy so he can tell himself he isn't being a bad boy. It's not your job to ease his guilt."

I needed Jeanie's words. More than that, I needed Jeanie, the same way she accused him of needing me: like a mommy, someone to tell me what to do. I'd needed this my whole life and was probably too eager to grasp at it.

"He's breaking the covenant of a long-term marriage. Don't you help him. Don't spend a minute in the same room with him."

That advice would've been easier to follow were my husband and I not still living under the same roof. Returning home night after night had passed the point of excruciating. Why was he still there? Why was I? Something in me kept rationalizing that men who ask for a divorce are expected to pack a bag and leave—but he'd never mentioned moving out and it didn't occur to me that maybe *I* should be the one packing. Along with my anger, my rational thinking was simply not engaged. I was invisible even to myself.

Getting home that evening after visiting with Jeanie, I found him friendly once more. He patted the couch next to him, inviting me to join him in watching the reality TV show *Survivor*.

*A game to see who outlasts the other?*

"No thanks," I said, heading for my room.

Trailing me, he asked in a small voice, "Have you, um, *told* anyone?"

Through Jeanie's eyes, I saw his question as a request for reassurance. Refusing to give it, I kept walking in silence, but I could feel him continuing after me.

"Um, because I haven't told anyone. My mom and dad . . . it'll break their hearts. This is going to hurt a lot of people . . ."

"*This* is going to hurt people?" I spun around. There I was. The strength of my voice sounded good to my ears. Robust. Solid. "It's not this, it's *you* . . . driving a bulldozer through our lives . . . *you* breaking your parents' hearts. It's not some random strike of lightning. It's *you*. Take responsibility."

I felt myself in my shoes, as if the substance of me had grown heavier and taller. Striding back to my room, I welcomed the surge of confidence. But once the bedroom door shut behind me, his timid, "Have you, um, told anyone?" gnawed at me because the truth was no, I hadn't told anyone. Other than Jeanie, I'd kept it all to myself.

*Why?*

My family would never forgive him.

*Am I protecting him from their judgment? Is my silence giving him a place to hide?*

Determined not to do that, I began the round of phone calls to my sisters. The reaction was immediate and strong.

Carla was the first to arrive. We spotted each other through the crowd at LAX and rushed to embrace, then drove south to check in to a spa.

In the sauna and again in the steam room, Carla asked the expected questions. Was he having an affair? Was it some midlife crisis?

"He's lucky Mom isn't alive," she declared with a snort.

That made me smile. I'd wondered which of my sisters would be the first to bring her up.

"If Mom were alive, he'd have had a stroke by now," I supposed.

"A heart attack," she countered.

Black-haired, fiery-eyed Mom had put the fear of Indian hexes into us. We grew up hearing stories of "the evil eye" and "bad medicine" and worse.

"Look out for Stick Indians," she warned us.

We were told Stick Indians lived invisibly in the woods, and could suddenly materialize to grab you if you were outside alone. And though medicine men could chant to heal the sick, they could just as easily do the opposite. Mom assured us she had her own "medicine" and if anyone crossed her, or one of her kids, they wouldn't be long for the world.

This was the extent of the spirituality I received from my parents. Superstitions? Those ran deep.

Her warnings followed us into early adulthood. When I was in my twenties, Mom got into an argument with a neighbor, the two going toe-to-toe in a shouting match. The next day's dawn was broken by the scream of sirens. An ambulance screeched to a halt in front of the neighbor's house. He had died of a heart attack.

"Definitely a heart attack," Carla said as we meandered through the resort gardens, imagining all the things Mom would do to my husband if she were alive.

We came back in from the pool and parted for our separate treatments. Mine was to be a body scrub, hers a massage.

The table felt warm beneath me as I stretched out, relaxing into it, still smiling at the fantasies of Mom's revenge. The therapist sprayed me with a hot mist and began to apply a salt scrub to my flesh. Her touch upon my skin exposed an ache deeper than I knew how to express.

*A touch—when will I be touched again?*

As she began rubbing my legs, I inhaled a few jerky breaths, fighting against tears. But my sorrow, without permission, unleashed itself. I wailed, crying the way Native American women do at a graveside, loudly and with absolute abandon. My sobs bounced off the white tile walls, and echoed through the spa. Curious people poked their heads in to investigate. What they saw was a weeping, naked lady, and a frozen massage therapist, her hose held like the Statue of Liberty's torch, uncertain what she'd done, or how she could undo it.

Carla dashed in.

"Don't worry," she said to the gathering staff. "Divorce. She's going through a divorce."

My little sister threw a towel over me and walked me out gently, as if holding broken bones together.


## Fracture

"The bone is broken!" Lilly hollers.

Lotta screams in terror and pain.

"Don't touch it," John orders. "Get back."

But we crowd in to see.

"Get back!" he yells.

The bone is visible, a jagged-looking pale thing peeking out from the bloody part of Lotta's twisted arm. John and Lilly repeat what we see.

"It's broken!"

Lotta twists in terror at the sight and the movement causes her to shriek louder.

"Don't move," Lilly cries. "Don't. Move."

Lotta fell off the banister on the staircase. I didn't see it, but heard the bang and bump of it, and the scream that followed. Like everyone else, I raced to the source of the sound and now here we stand, a helpless circle around our sister. There's no grown-up to fix it, and though John and Lilly are the Boss, they can do nothing. None of us can. We know it isn't the type of hurt that will just go away, like the time a bee sting turned Lotta's hand into a balloon. This time, we can't pretend everything's OK.

Her cries define our long day. Lotta grows silent only occasionally, in exhaustion, until a slight jostle sends her back into agony. Witnesses, we remain at attention near her. We don't play. We don't fight. We don't know what to do. At last, Dad comes home and lifts Lotta in his arms. Despite the jarring of her limb required by the move, she barely whimpers. She must be out of tears, I think.

In a hush, we stand like an honor guard as Dad carries her out of the house to take her to a doctor. When the door shuts behind them, we collapse: John onto a chair, Lilly to a staircase step, the rest of us to the floor, as if our own bones just gave out.

## Hex

Carlotta called several days later, after Carla had already left town. I was taking a curve on Sunset Boulevard when my cell phone rang.

"It's done," she announced.

A smile immediately parted my lips. Days earlier, when she'd heard my news, she had offered up the expected.

"He's lucky Mom's not alive. He'd be dead by now."

"I know, I know," I had sighed, chuckling at the way our family tends to think alike in the midst of trauma.

That day, Carlotta declared the worst revenge she could imagine. "I'll send a bone crusher hex."

Now, here she was, letting me know she'd made good on the vow. "What happened?"

"I was out praying at sunrise. Far on the horizon, there was a bird that I thought was really small. But as it got closer, I saw it was gigantic. It was flying right at me, descending as it flew."

I pictured her on a windswept Nebraska plain, watching the silhouette of the bird against the sunrise. Carlotta, in her hardhat, would have gotten up very early for her job erecting wind turbines. The girl who once tumbled off a staircase banister now made her living suspended high up in the air, assembling the tall towers that spin in the wind.

"It was an eagle." Carlotta paused to let that sink in.

*An eagle.*

"When it got to me, I had the strangest sensation; like it was there just for me." Carlotta's voice lifted in wonderment. "I smiled up at him and said, 'Break his bones.' And you know what? The eagle dipped down and did a complete circle in the air right above me, and then took off like an arrow to the south. So, just wait," she wrapped up, her voice chipper again. "Broken bones are on the way." Her light laughter suggested she was only teasing, offering up a tale to make a spurned wife feel better.

That night at home, I thought about the legacy of "Indian medicine." I couldn't say I actually believed in hexes. They were part of the fertile stew we grew up with: Stick Indians, the magic of Coyote, meadowlarks speaking Nez Perce, the absolute blessing of an eagle overhead. I learned that the dead do visit, premonitions are to be heeded, cars and other inanimate objects can be "jinxed," and of course, Natives are capable of communicating over great distances, often through dreams. In adulthood, I hadn't stopped to debate any of these ideas. They just fell away as my life enlarged first to college and then to a career as a news reporter. But had they really gone? Somewhere in a drawer, I still owned a little buckskin pouch, my medicine bag, meant to keep me safe. It was in a bundle with three or four eagle feathers. *And sage*, I thought, jumping up to look for the stick of dried sage, tied tight with red yarn. As I searched, I remembered a time early in my marriage when I thought Coyote seemed to be speaking to me.

It was back when I'd first built the cabin in Montana. We were living in New York then, and were about to fly west for a week in the wilderness. The night before our trip, I dreamed three coyotes were yipping at the moon as they stood atop the cliff in front of my cabin. The scene was so vivid, their howls so primal, that the dream left a lingering impression upon me.

Hiking in Montana days later, we happened to climb the very hill I had dreamed about, careful of the slippery shale at the bottom and the patches of snow at the top. At the peak, I spotted coyote tracks in the dusty bare areas and in the snow along the ridge.

"Hey, my dream is true," I declared, crouching down to examine the tracks. "Look, coyote tracks. Remember the dream I told you about? Remember?"

Getting no answer, I turned and saw that he was several steps away and had his back to me. He was urinating. Unconsciously, my eyes followed the arc of the thin spray and I noticed it landing on more tracks in the snow, turning the coyote footprints into little puddles of yellow.

I stepped back in horror and almost lost my footing on the cliff. Yet I said nothing about his disrespect, because it had been unintentional, right? A guy needing to relieve himself after a climb

43

up a steep hill wasn't so unusual. *And he isn't Native American,* I reasoned. *How would he know?* Still, his peeing where Coyote had spoken to me in a dream so disconcerted me that I descended in silence.

A pack of coyotes slipped noiselessly down the ridge that night, perhaps tracing the scent of the urine. They prowled outside the cabin, pacing quietly at first, until one howled, and then another. Their cries built upon each other to a sound both threatening and mournful. I listened in the dark while the man next to me slept on, unaware.

# Chapter 4

As the uncomfortably undefined days dragged on, I felt as suspended as Carlotta must have been before losing her hold on the bannister. Neither he nor I had taken action on the divorce, and though I wanted more than anything to disappear from that house and the confusing life within it, I held on, gripping with all my might. What I was clutching on to, or what I feared might await me at the bottom if I let go, was never clear.

One night, I woke up with the abrupt recollection that Halloween was three days away. My daughter and her family lived out of state, and flying there to trick-or-treat with my grandson was our annual tradition. I'd booked the flight weeks prior but, in the fog of these days, it had slipped my mind.

I looked at the clock.

It was two in the morning. My flight was less than twenty-four hours away, and I'd forgotten to get a costume. I fell back against the pillow, upset at myself. My grandson, Phoenix, loved guessing what his Grammie might be, and in years past, had squealed with delight when I popped in as Tinker Bell, or Cat in the Hat. Now, those memories felt like a relic from someone else's life. I tossed in bed, knowing that coming up with a costume was just the start of what the weekend required. I would have to tell the child that his grandfather was leaving. A surge of anger made me fling the covers away, as if I were slapping away the monstrous man.

*Monster . . .*

I sprang from bed, alive with an idea. Flipping on the light switch and swinging open the closet door, I spotted it. There, stored in a box high on the upper shelf. Climbing up on a chair, I was able to reach it and carefully set the box on the bed, where I tentatively peeled back the tissue paper to reveal the white lace of my wedding gown. Perfect. High neck, long sleeve, a Victorian style.

My hands trembled as I lifted it overhead and slipped my arms into the sleeves. It still fit. Heart skipping, I turned to face the mirror. An untamed bride, with messy dark hair and swollen red eyes above a crazed smile, peered back at me. Electric with energy, I let out a laugh.

Ten days ago, life as I knew it had ended and I'd been ghost-walking ever since. But now I was wildly awake. Tingling with fury, I admired the fierce bride in the mirror.

*You want to divorce me? You want to divorce* me?

Robert De Niro's taxi driver came to mind: "You talkin' to me?" At that, I buckled in uncontrollable laughter, observing the reflected bride bend at the waist, sink against the wall, and heave at the comedy of it.

*Yes, I have a Halloween costume. I am the Bride of Frankenstein.*

The image in the mirror applauded my choice of costume.

When I got to Albuquerque the next day, I didn't tell my grandson the news. I put on a happy face, not wanting to ruin his Halloween. But seven-year-old Phoenix seemed to gather that something wasn't right. As I stood listless in the kitchen, he approached with a large stuffed toy, the cartoon character Shrek.

"Punch it," he said. "You'll feel better."

*How did you know?*

Touched by his empathy, I took the Shrek and gave it a light slap.

"No, like this," he said, as he pummeled it.

I smiled, and joined in. We punched, wrestled, karate chopped, and stomped on it until we both fell over in sweet exhaustion. My magical grandson offered me better medicine than any high-priced therapist. He gave me permission to beat up the ogre.

Later that night came the unveiling.

"OK, ready!" my daughter Lizzie called. It was the moment we revealed our costumes to each other. Phoenix bounded out of his room dressed as Austin Powers in a red velvet suit and white frilly collar. Lizzie emerged from her room with a tall blue wig, red beads around her neck and the lime green dress of Marge Simpson. From the bathroom, I walked into the living room to face them. Lizzie jumped.

"Mom," she whispered, "your wedding dress?"

"She's a bride," Phoenix announced with the simplicity of a child. My white lace matched the lace on his shirt. He looked pleased.

"Yes, I am. I'm the Bride of . . . Frankenstein," I explained.

My daughter looked doubtful.

"Just wait," I promised. "We have to stop at the store and get some hairspray, but once I rat up my hair and spray on some white stripes, it'll be perfect."

I walked tentatively, pulling the delicate train behind me.

"It's going to be great," I continued, not very convincingly. My middle-of-the-night decision to mock my humiliation had seemed wildly right at the time, but in practice it felt precarious, like glass that could shatter.

"Awesome," Lizzie finally said. "Cool."

Her eyes told me she got it, but because of the child in the room, neither of us said more. For Phoenix, the gown was simply part of his favorite holiday—getting dressed up to get candy.

"Let's go," he said, walking with an Austin Powers swagger to the door.

Later, in a strip mall parking lot, I closed my eyes against the hairspray. White gook rose in streaks from my temples to the top of my ratted hair. Phoenix was about ten feet away, sipping punch from a plastic pouch, waiting for Grammie to finish her transformation. I'd applied white-grey makeup to my face, and used a black pencil to arch my brows. I looked as deadly as I felt. Marge Simpson paced nearby. Our trick or treating was about to begin.

"You look spooky," Phoenix complimented.

As he approached, his foot slipped. In his stumble, he inadvertently squeezed the juice pouch in his hand. A spray of red liquid spurted from the thin straw, landing on my gown.

*My wedding dress.*

"Phoenix!" I snapped.

Tiny spots of red grew as the liquid spread through the lace.

"Be careful," I shrieked.

"Get back here," Lizzie ordered him.

I lost myself. My hands lifted the lovely fabric to examine the red bleeding into the white.

"I didn't mean it. It was an accident."

The small voice of my grandson brought me back. As if from afar, I saw the three of us in that dreary parking lot, dressed bizarrely, frozen in torment, and washed by the golden orange of a desert sunset. Phoenix's face showed fear and confusion. My heart swelled for him, bringing me fully out of my trance.

"It's OK, Phoenix." I exhaled. "It's just a costume."

He stared back at me uncertainly.

"Maybe it's even *better* now," I said, releasing the gown from my hand and the red splatters from my sight. "Let's pretend it's blood," I suggested. "That makes it even more Halloween scary, don't you think?"

He remained immobile.

"I'm sorry I snapped at you."

I held my arms open for him.

"I'm so sorry."

He trudged to me. We hugged, until Lizzie called us to the car.

On a mesa outside the city, we visited the homes in my daughter's subdivision, a development so new some streets didn't have sidewalks. Occasionally, I glanced down at the gown that had once been worn at an elegant penthouse ceremony in Manhattan as it dragged through the desert dirt. Without effort, my eyes were ghostly. Without intention, I walked like a dead bride. When a group of teenagers passed, one tossed off a compliment: "Cool Bride of Frankenstein."

Later, after Phoenix was in bed, I tossed the dress in the garbage can.

## Ghosts

Carla hands me a beer bottle. Our little hands struggle with the "church key," until at last the bottle opener works and the top pops off. It rolls across on the floor and Baby chases it.

"Quick, before they wake up," I urge.

We race to the kitchen sink to pour the beer down the drain and fill the bottle with water.

"Hurry, get the cap back on."

Carla goes after Baby to retrieve the cap, but Lotta's already taken it from her and now Baby starts to cry.

"Shhh. You'll wake them."

Carla pries the bottle cap from Lotta's fist and runs back to me. "Hurry!"

She hands the cap to me and we line it up on top of the beer bottle. I press with all my might but it doesn't snap back on.

"Push harder."

"I am."

"Stand back. Let me try."

"Let's both push."

We put the beer bottle on the floor and take turns pushing down on the cap but it refuses to pop back into place.

"Maybe they won't notice."

We carry the beer bottle of water back to the living room and slide it back into its slot in the open case of beer on the floor. The top of the bottle looks slightly tilted.

Mom's snore makes us freeze. She seems to choke for half a second before going back to regular breathing.

"Quick, let's pour out another one. Come on, before they wake up. Hurry."

Mom and Dad, asleep on the couch, are oblivious of us running back and forth to the kitchen in our frenzied but failed effort to cure drunkenness by substituting water for beer.

We can't cure it.

# Chapter 5

Day of the Dead skeletons danced in the store windows, making a mockery of my task.

It was time to tell my grandson. I parked in front of an Albuquerque café and turned off the ignition. Maybe it was the extra time I took before turning toward him or the way I breathed deeply before suggesting, too cheerily, that we go in for hot chocolate.

"So you can tell me about your personal life?" he asked.

*Had Lizzie given him a hint? Or was he just reading my mind, as he sometimes seemed to do?*

Once we were seated and had ordered our drinks, I began.

"I want to tell you something that's happening."

"What?"

"Well," I paused. "Adults sometimes do stupid things."

He nodded, almost impatient at such an obvious statement.

"Well, right now, your Grandpa is doing something very stupid and he's making a big mistake."

"What's he doing?"

"He doesn't want to be my husband anymore."

"What?"

Phoenix set down his cup. His little face contorted.

I repeated myself.

"He wants a *divorce*?"

The color on my grandson's face vanished as I nodded.

We sat quietly. He looked around the room as if nothing were recognizable.

"I thought you were going to say he's doing drugs," he whispered.

"Why?"

"You said he was being stupid and making a mistake. Doing drugs is being stupid and making a mistake. We learned about it in school."

"Oh, you're right."

A few moments passed.

"Why does he want a divorce?" he asked, looking into my eyes again.

"I don't know. Maybe he feels old and wants to be young again."

"But age has nothing to do with marriage," exclaimed the child.

"You're right."

Light snow drifted past the café windows. We were the only customers left. I reached over and held his hand.

After a moment, his voice croaked, "Grammie? Is he leaving us because he doesn't like someone in our family?"

I cringed that this child might feel responsible. My brother John was forty when he told me that, as a six-year-old, he blamed himself for Mom and Dad's drinking. That the youngest carry the world's wrongs was a wound I couldn't allow this time.

"No. No, don't think that, Phoenix. It's not because of me, or you, or your mom, or anyone in our family."

Phoenix held a hard stare. I could sense his distress.

"No, Phoenix," I went on. "He's not leaving because of any of us. He's leaving because he's afraid of getting old."

"What? Afraid of getting old?"

Phoenix raised his hands to his cheeks in disbelief. To him, "getting old" was a goal. When he was six, he wanted to be eight. Now, he couldn't wait to be ten.

"Yep," I said, "afraid of getting old. Sometimes, when men get close to sixty, they want to be twenty."

"But that's crazy . . . afraid of getting old?"

"Yeah."

*Adults* are *crazy*, I thought, *and ever hurtful to the little ones entrusted to them.*

# Chapter 6

On my flight back to Los Angeles, it took an extra shove to squish my carry-on bag between others in the overhead. I too had to squeeze into place. An oversized passenger spilled out of the aisle seat, and an unaccompanied minor had the window, which left me the center. I tried making myself as small as possible, contained and collected. And the reality of returning to my life on the other side of this flight pressed in on me.

As we ascended, the impossible blue of the New Mexico sky caught my eye, reassuring me with its brilliance. But as we banked, the dead brown desert below came into view. I leaned back, and closed my eyes against this journey back to the unknown. Divorce in my fifties wasn't a destination I'd expected. I didn't have an itinerary for it, or a bag packed with the essentials it might require. If I could have somehow prevented the plane from ever arriving at our destination, I would have. The thought of what awaited me was crushing.

I thought, *This is where faith surely makes things easier for people brave enough to trust it*. I'd interviewed people who were standing on their blackened property after a wildfire, or whose child had been kidnapped, or whose husband was killed at war—and they'd said something like, "My faith will get me through." They credited *faith* for the courage to walk on and trust—but trust what, exactly? That things will just somehow work out? That wayward husbands will come to their senses?

I had no such faith. I'd been making my own way, fending for myself, and relying on good ol' self-determination ever since I could remember. Within me was a fighter, though I'd lost sight of her.

## Choose Bravery

It's 1972, in Minneapolis.

"Um, there's been a lot of Indian news lately," the radio man says, shifting from foot to foot, apparently unnerved by the sullen brown faces staring back at him. There are about thirty of us Indian students in our makeshift headquarters. Almost everyone has long dark hair, worn braided or hanging loose, a few with a red bandana tied across their forehead as a headband. In green army jackets or in buckskin fringe coats, we are plopped onto an old couch, or sitting on the floor, the windowsill, the top of a battered desk. One guy in dark glasses rocks his folding chair backward.

"Because of all the marches and protests . . . with AIM and all . . . " the radio man stammers on. AIM is the militant American Indian Movement. Half the people in the room are members.

"We thought we'd give you . . . uh, you students . . . five minutes a day for Indian News . . . you know, kind of a daily radio recap."

The radio man's body seems to fall in on itself in apparent exhaustion at having to make a pitch to such a stony crowd. My body, however, perks up. Indian News? A daily broadcast?

I glance around at the others in the room, thinking that surely someone will jump at the chance to be on the air. But the faces remain impassive, giving no hint that they even heard his offer.

"Anyone interested?" he asks.

Silence.

"It wouldn't be volunteering. It would be an actual job, part-time. You'd get paid two and half hours a day to put together the five-minute broadcast."

I look left and right in disbelief that no one is raising a hand to grab the job. I certainly can't take it. I'm only a freshman, and at seventeen, much younger than everyone else. But somebody should do this.

"Anyone?" he asks.

"I'll do it," I hear my voice say. I don't remember flinging it skyward, but there is my hand, raised overhead. "I'll do it."

The next day I am on the air with Indian News.

I choose bravery and it exhilarates me.

*That was the first step of my career*, I thought, opening my eyes once again to the crowded airplane. My whole life changed because I took a leap. Of faith. By raising my hand and trying something, I had launched a career. *So, journeys into the unknown aren't all bad*, I reasoned. To fortify that thought, I recalled other instances of pushing past obstacles, like the day I was just getting started in TV news. I'd complained to the assignment editor that only male reporters were being sent to Mt. St. Helens.

"OK," he said. "You want to cover the volcano? Sign here."

The paper he handed me was a release, absolving both the station and the US government of the responsibility of searching for my body in the event of an eruption.

I rolled my eyes, signed the form, and got on TV the next time the mountain bellowed.

*Yes*, I thought, gazing out the airplane window, *I've ventured out of my comfort zone before. I can do it again.* Yet, this was different. I hadn't raised my hand and volunteered for this assignment or signed any forms, willingly taking on the challenge of being divorced and alone at this age. Who could blame me for being terrified?

*Terrified. That's it. I am afraid.*

The part of me so paralyzed by the events of these days cracked at the insight. I took deep breaths, acknowledging my fright.

*I've been afraid to let myself feel . . . fear.*

I was so relieved to finally have a name for the feeling that I almost tapped the overweight guy next to me to announce: "It's fear. That's what it is."

Recognizing my fear, I became conscious of the question fueling it: *Who's going to take care of me?* It was an age-old question in this little girl's heart. I needed a guide to tell me where we were going and to promise me we'd make it safely.


## Journey

"We're leaving."

"How come?"

"Be quiet. Hold hands. Stick together." Those are the only answers John and Lilly give. We are leaving the Projects, on foot. John herds us down the sidewalk. Lilly carries Lotta. Annie holds Baby. I have Carla's hand tight in mine.

"Where are we going?"

"Shush, keep walking."

"Why are we walking?"

*Maybe it's because the mush ran out,* I think. *Or maybe they know where Mom and Dad are, and we're going to get them. Or maybe . . .*

My thoughts are stopped by the rushing heat of a bus pulling up to the curb.

John and Lilly push us toward it.

"Get on."

"Hurry, get on the bus."

We lift the little ones on and then clamber up after them. The folding door swooshes closed behind us. Before I can turn back from looking at the door, the floor tips and jostles me into Carla, who falls into Carlotta.

"Grab Lotta. Get up."

Lilly and John order us about.

"Get a seat. Move over. You sit there. Hold her on your lap."

I stare out the window at everything flying past. The bus turns and the Projects vanish. The trees outside the windows become bigger and greener the farther we drive. We come down a long hill, and suddenly water replaces the trees. We cross a bridge and now the water stretches out to meet the grey sky. Caught up by the sight, I forget to ask where we're going and how come we're going.

When the bus stops, I stand to get out.

"Not yet. Sit down!"

People get off and others get on. I study their clothes and shoes and shopping bags, looking so hard that I don't notice when the water disappears. Outside the bus, there are buildings now and people on sidewalks.

"We're downtown," John says. "We have to transfer here."

"What's transfer?" Annie pipes up.

"Just get off the bus," Lilly says. With a rising voice, she calls, "Quick, before the door closes. All of you, come on. Hurry!"

We drop down onto the sidewalk, where it's so loud that we grab hands, as if that might make it quieter. Lilly, breathing deeply, counts us and pushes us into a tight circle. John turns his head back and forth, left and right, looking up and down the street.

"This way," he decides.

"Stick together," Lilly commands. "Don't get lost."

*Lost?*

I maneuver myself to make sure I stay between Lilly and John. Getting lost from them is the scariest thing I can imagine.

"Where are we going?" I ask.

No one answers.

"How come we're downtown?" I try again.

We climb a steep hill.

"Puh-eye . . . Pike," Annie announces.

I don't know what she's talking about, so she points to the street sign.

"Pike," she repeats.

I still don't know what she means.

"Pike Street. It's where we are, stupid."

"Oh."

Our troop comes to a stop on Pike Street, where the oldest look around for a while, like they misplaced something. A store window catches my eye. There are toys inside.

"No, you can't go in," John says. "No, you can't go to the bathroom. Just wait."

"Is this our bus?" Lilly interrupts.

"Must be," he says. "Come on, everyone. Let's go, let's go."

We jostle up the stairs of another bus. Since it's our second ride, we're not as jumpy as we were the first time. We settle into our seats. The heater feels good after the cold, loud Pike Street, or maybe it's the comfort of sitting, or the low hum of the engine, or the slight rocking back and forth. Whatever it is, it makes us nod off; first Baby, then Lotta and Carla, then me.

"Last stop," snaps the bus driver, waking us. "Everyone off. End of the line."

"But, but . . ." John almost shrieks. "It's not the right place."

He and Lilly leap up to talk to the driver, while Annie and I gather the Kids into a huddle in the aisle. The bus is empty except for us.

"Sorry," the driver says. "You've got to get out."

The bus abandons us. We are seven kids in the wrong place. At first, no one says anything. Lilly's lower lip quivers, and she turns away from us.

"How come we're here?" I ask.

Annie gives me a mean look so I shut up. I follow her eyes. She's watching John, who is giving Lilly an apologetic look but she doesn't see it because her back is to us. She's taking deep breaths.

"I'm hungry," Carla starts.

"Shhh," I hiss at her.

Lilly takes some steps away from us. The prospect that she might actually cry rattles me. The Boss can't cry. It's so unnerving that I unconsciously reach for Annie's hand. She must be shaken too, because for a second, she lets me take it. We're too young to appreciate the planning John and Lilly must have done for this journey; the days, or maybe weeks, of scrounging up nickels and dimes for bus fare; the weighing of the dangers in the ordeal; the overcoming of their fears. We don't know anything about their calculations. We know only that Lilly looks chillingly close to tears, and we are held still by the sight.

Suddenly, John grabs our attention. In a deep voice, meant to sound certain and calm, he says, "We're just going to have to walk."

At that, Lilly exhales and snaps back to herself. With authority, she turns to us. "Start walking, kids."

Reassured, we fall in behind her and John, the leaders of our scraggly group. Annie looks down at our clasped hands, and tosses mine back to me like it's a dead lizard.

It is hours since we left the Projects. We traipse, toddle, and trudge, while exchanging Baby back and forth, lifting up, setting down, falling behind, and trying to keep up. We pass houses with pretty green yards. Sometimes, there are children playing in those yards who stop their games to watch us go by.

In time, complaints pop forth from Annie, me, Carla, or Lotta. Our laments overlap, and always get the same answer.

"I know you're hungry. We're all hungry," Lilly says.

Block after block we walk.

"This is Buh-ee-a . . ." Annie begins.

60

"Beacon," John finishes for her. "Beacon Avenue. We're not supposed to be on Beacon. We're supposed to be on Rainier. We got on the wrong bus."

"We have to walk the entire length of Beacon Hill," Lilly sighs.

"Where are we going?" I remember to ask.

Maybe because they're exhausted, they finally answer.

"Aunt Teddy's."

Aunt Teddy. I smile. *Aunt Teddy*, I think with each footstep. Knowing our destination makes the going easier. That is until Carla brings us to a halt with a sudden wail.

"Don't cry," Lilly urges. "I know you're tired. But please, don't cry."

It's no use. Carla cries with her mouth wide open and her eyes squeezed shut. She won't take another step. Her bawling is the loudest thing on the street.

Lilly can't lift her up because she has Baby in her arms. Carla's too big for me or Annie to carry for more than a step or two. John, holding Lotta, turns away so Lotta won't see Carla crying and copy her. But crying is contagious and just hearing Carla makes Lotta gulp and sniff. Baby's next. A yelp. A sob.

"No crying!" Lilly demands, but it's no use. We are stopped at the mercy of three-year-old Carla.

"Crying will slow us down," John mutters, stepping away from us. Abruptly, he turns back with a bright face. "Hey kids, how about we put on a show? It's a marching show and we get to sing. 'The ants go marching one by one, hurrah, hurrah . . .' Come on, let's sing."

Putting on shows is one of our favorite things. John often has us put on shows at home, where we sing and play different parts. But we've never put on a show on a sidewalk after taking two busses to the wrong place.

"Come on, let's march," he suggests with a sunny smile, his eyes open wide, his chin nodding up and down.

Lilly starts marching, lifting each knee high. Annie copies her, and so do I. Carla sniffles and trudges forward.

"Sing together," John says. "Ready? Sing as we march, now. The ants go marching one by one, hurrah, hurrah. The ants go marching one by one, hurrah, hurrah. The ants go marching one by one, the little one stops to suck her thumb, and they all go marching down to the earth, to get out of the rain, boom, boom, boom, boom."

We laugh, because Baby is the little one, and she does suck her thumb. We march and wonder what his next verse will be.

"The ants go marching two by two . . ."

It's almost dark when we finally march down the far end of Beacon Hill.

". . . and they all go marching . . . down . . . to the earth . . . to get out . . . of the rain . . ."

At the bottom of the hill the houses fall away and are replaced by busy boulevards and the roar of traffic.

"Everyone hold hands."

There are multiple lanes of cars flying fast in both directions. John and Lilly arrange us at the curb, like it's a starting line.

"Ready, set . . . No! Wait, wait."

A car whips past.

"OK, no one go until I say . . . RUN."

We sprint, our tired legs pumping as hard as they can, and make it across the boulevard. Gasping, the biggest kids smile at each other in victory. I grin wide so they'll notice I'm one of them. A few blocks ahead, another busy avenue stops us. Cars and trucks zip past.

"This is Rainier Avenue," John announces. "We're almost there."

"No crying, now." Lilly looks each of us in the eye. "Hold hands. Ready, everyone? . . . Ready? . . . RUN!"

We race.

It is our finish line, after seven miles on foot.

Panting for breath, Lilly points and says, "I think that's the one."

"Yeah, that's it," gasps John. "The blue and white apartment building. We're here. We're here."

Excited, they pick up the pace. I grab Carla's hand to pull her along. We climb some stairs to a landing that has several doors along it.

"This one," John says, and gives it a tap.

We shrink into each other until we are all touching in some way, holding hands, an arm over a shoulder, a little one hoisted on a hip, a head leaning against a leg. United, we fix our eyes on the door, willing it to open.

John knocks again, louder this time.

As one, we hold our breath.

A latch clicks, the door swings open, and there is Aunt Teddy.

"Oh, kids!" she exclaims.

Relief almost knocks us over.

Our aunt smiles and looks past us in expectation of Mom or Dad.

"They're not . . . here . . ." John stammers.

"Just us," Lilly croaks.

"Oh. Kids," Teddy repeats, but in a different tone. It is still welcoming but there's a grand understanding in it. Her eyes take in our state.

"Oh, kids," she says for the third time. "Come in."

But we can't, because the door is blocked by John and Lilly collapsing into Teddy. They keep their arms around her for a long time, hiding their faces against her, while she pats their shoulders saying, "It's OK. It's all right. Everything's going to be OK." Gradually, I realize they're crying, and it stuns me but doesn't terrify me. I guess it's OK for the Boss to cry because we're at Teddy's now. Maybe the rules are different here, or maybe Aunt Teddy is the Boss now. We stand on the landing waiting until twelve-year-old John and ten-year-old Lilly are done hiding their tears against Teddy. Finally, our huddle moves into her apartment, where there is food and water, a bathroom, a warm place to sleep, and someone to take care of us, for a few days at least.

# Chapter 7

"I love you," he said, startling me.

My suitcase was still in hand as I stood in the foyer, just getting home from my trip to Albuquerque.

"I want to hold you," he continued.

The door hadn't yet closed behind me, and there he was professing love. No wonder I couldn't get my footing. Nothing at home made sense.

"People who love each other don't do this to each other," I answered flatly, dropping my bag to the floor and moving past him. His posture shifted and his expression hardened.

"I'm going to Montana this weekend," he blurted, setting off an alarm in my head.

*Montana is my place. The cabin is mine.*

"I want to get some of my stuff," he said in a measured voice. "Just get a few things, my guns, the ATV, whatever else is there."

"You do not have permission to enter my cabin," I said, slowly.

"I have a lawyer," he warned.

*He has a lawyer. I need a lawyer. This is a divorce. We are adversaries.*

Like the gears of a machine suddenly engaging and clanging to life, the process was under way. As I turned toward my bedroom, I heard him say, "My flight's in the morning."

The alarm bells in my head became sirens blaring so loudly my body shook. It was the awakening of my guard.


## Wakes Us in the Dark

Cuckoo, cuckoo, cuckoo.

The clock is alive again. We never know when it might cuckoo, or when it might stop.

Cuckoo, cuckoo . . .

It's like an alarm set to its own wandering time.

Cuckoo . . .

It wakes us in the dark of night. Crowded together in bed, my sisters and I count the cuckoos. Thirty-one, thirty-two, thirty-three. We know the clock's supposed to chime the hour, but it went mad long ago. The little bird comes out and cuckoos whenever it wants. Days pass without a peep. Other times, it can't control itself.

Cuckoo, cuckoo, cuckoo . . .

Birds. Somehow, nutty birds accompany us kids.

John brings home a parakeet.

We don't have food to eat, but we have a parakeet in a cage and a clock on the wall that can't stop cuckooing. This time the clock gets to forty-one cuckoos before it stops, a new record. Gradually, we girls drift back to sleep, elbows and feet entangled; three of us with our heads at the foot of the mattress, the other three in the opposite direction. Because he's a boy, John gets his own room that he shares with the parakeet.

One day, he comes home with a record from the school library that's supposed to teach the bird to talk. He plays it all day. "Hel-looooo baaaby, want a kiss? Hellooooooo baaaby, want a kiss?" The voice on the record is a man's deep baritone that sinks low at the elongated end of "Hellooooo" but rises quickly and comically high on "want a kiss?" We laugh and mimic the voice.

The parakeet doesn't learn to talk. It escapes from its cage and flutters about the house, causing us to duck. It perches on the rod where a curtain would hang, if we owned one, and drops poop on the windowsill. Once in a while we try to catch it with a towel or a sheet but it darts above us, leaving us shrieking and ducking for cover.

Cuckoo, cuckoo, cuckoo . . .

Hellooooo baaaby, want a kiss?

The cuckoo clock bird is always startling in its unpredictability, screaming at a houseful of kids whose nerves are already badly frayed. It jolts us every time.

## Another Crashing Noise

A sound woke me. I sat up, immediately alert, and listened in the dark. My heart began to pound. I remembered how he used to drill me on what to do if there were a prowler. First, I was supposed to get the gun from his nightstand, then call 911. Slowly, I scooted my body to his side of the bed and reached into the drawer where he kept the pistol.

*It's not here.*

Another crashing noise made me leap from bed.

*Get a grip, Hattie. You've covered way too many crime stories. You're getting paranoid.*

I switched on the patio light. Shivering, I peeked through the sheer curtain, and saw tree branches tossing to and fro.

*The wind. Relax.*

A branch must have broken loose and fallen to the ground.

Lying back on my pillow, I pondered my jumpiness. The gun was gone, but that didn't mean anything sinister. Did it? I hardly knew what to think about anything. In time, I fell back asleep. The next day, work consumed me and I didn't consider any of it until I returned home to find a phone message from Montana in which he again proclaimed his love. He was the cuckoo clock, disorienting

66

me again. I didn't know what was true and wanting to believe him, I convinced myself that I was the crazy one.

When he returned home, I told him about the incident of my fright in the middle of the night and how I'd looked for the gun but couldn't find it.

"Oh," he laughed, nervously. "I didn't want you to have a weapon."

"I'm not going to commit suicide over this," I said, annoyed at his presumption.

"I wasn't worried about *that*," he replied, looking at his feet and shifting awkwardly. "I was afraid you might shoot *me*."

I stared at him in disbelief, feeling the tiniest kernel sprout within me. It was the seed of dislike.

He stepped into the guest room briefly and returned with a .38 revolver extended to me in his palm.

"Here," he chirped. "You can have this one. Know how to use it?"

He demonstrated how to hold, load, and aim the gun.

"Remember your stance," he encouraged, spreading his legs rigid like a cop about to break through a door.

I played along as the man who was afraid I might shoot him put a loaded weapon into my hands.

"Remember how to reload?"

"Yep," I answered.

"OK, you keep the .38 in your room. I'll keep the Glock in my room." He smiled, pulling out a semi-automatic 9 mm pistol.

I sucked in my breath. We were now both holding guns and standing just a few feet from each other.

"You know what?" he said. "Maybe we better phone each other, anytime we're on our way home, so neither of us thinks the other is an intruder."

"Oh. Good idea."

I backed away. It was time to find a divorce lawyer.

# Chapter 8

"The Lord is my shepherd."

After speaking those words slowly, Aunt Teddy pauses and nods at me in encouragement.

"The Lord is my shep-ward," I repeat back to her.

I don't know what it means, or why she wants me to learn that sentence, but since the journey we kids took to her apartment, Aunt Teddy says it all the time, even after she brought us home. Mom and Dad are still gone, so Teddy is staying with us for a while. She cooks. We eat. And we climb all over her whenever she sits down on the couch.

Yet miraculously at this moment, there is no one else around but me. I have Teddy all to myself. The other kids must be downstairs or outside playing. She is picking up clothes off the floor of the bedroom when I wander in. Seeing me, she smiles, sits on the edge of the mattress, and says her favorite sentence.

"The Lord is my shepherd."

"The Lord is my shep-ard," I echo carefully.

"I shall not want," she adds.

"I shall not want what?"

"Just, I shall not want." She grins.

"I shall not want," I repeat, looking down at my bare feet, and then back up to Teddy's face. She is my dad's sister and has white skin like him. Her light brown hair curls around her ears, barely touching her collar, which is crisp and clean. Her clothes are always ironed, I notice.

"He maketh me to lie down in green pastures," she prompts.

"How come?"

"First, try saying the words. And then, I'll tell you."

"He maketh . . . I can't remember."

"He maketh me to lie down in green pastures."

"How come they're green?"

"A green pasture is a good one. It means it's full of food for you. Now try it. He maketh me to lie down in green pastures."

"He maketh me to lie down in green pastures," I repeat.

"He leadeth me beside still waters."

An image of the water I glimpsed from the bus window comes to mind.

"He leadeth me beside still waters," she says again, pulling my attention back to her.

"What is 'leadeth'?"

"It means leads, the way a shepherd leads his sheep."

"How come he's leading me to water?"

She gives me the kind of smile that makes me feel like I'm growing taller right before her.

"Everyone needs water to live," she explains. "And it's not just any water. Listen to the words, 'He leadeth me beside *still* waters.' That means it's not stormy seas, or wild waves, but still water, where you'll be safe."

"Where you'll be safe," I repeat, thinking it's the next line.

She shakes her head at me, and says, "He restoreth my soul."

"He what?"

## Lead Me, Please

Jeanie had advised me to meet with three divorce lawyers before deciding which one to hire. From various friends, I got referrals, and from some, disavowals. "Never hire that guy!" Eventually, with the list narrowed to three, I walked into my first appointment resolved not to make any decisions until I'd met with each one.

"How can I help you?" the first attorney asked. She was middle-aged, with untamed hair, manicured nails, and intent eyes.

"Well, you know, this might be a mistake." I faltered right off the top, suddenly doubting the whole thing. "I'm not even positive I need a lawyer."

"Does your husband want a divorce?" she asked, all business.

I nodded.

"Is he having an affair?"

I began to shake my head no, then stopped to stare at her, wide-eyed. Her firmness was the opposite of my flakiness.

"Um, he says he wants mediation," I said, thinking she'd take this as a good sign.

"They always want mediation when they've got something to hide." She waved her hand, as if batting an invisible fly.

"Well, uh . . ." I glanced down at my wedding ring. "I don't want a fight."

"What, exactly, did he say?" she persisted.

"He said the only thing we own together is the house, and that we should sell it, split the money, and be done."

"How long have you been married?"

"Seventeen years."

"Oh, sweetheart, you own more than half a house. You own half a partnership in his business, if he has one, and half of anything he and his partners have purchased, like real estate. Is there any?"

"A building in Beverly Hills . . . but I don't want to go to court. I don't want a divorce. I . . . I . . . I'm not sure he's thinking clearly."

"Listen, *you* are not thinking clearly," she said. "Pay attention."

My eyes, which had been darting about for an escape, were caught by hers.

"Don't sign with a realtor. Don't put that house up for sale."

This wasn't what I wanted to hear. I wanted to move. Living under the same roof made me feel like I was losing my mind, getting paranoid, retreating into myself.

"Dear, you're not in a position to make any decisions because you can't think clearly. You are in shock. Do you understand?"

She took my hands in hers, talking to me like I'd just been pulled out of a burning building.

"You are in shock. If you remember *anything* from our meeting today, remember this: don't move out of that house. Don't *sign* a thing. Nothing. Heck, don't even sign with me."

Whether it was the "sweetheart," the "dear," or the holding of my hands, she had me.

"You're hired," I exhaled. "Where do I sign?"

Embracing me, she laughed and handed me the retainer contract. I would sign anything if it meant having someone to shelter me.


## Valley of the Shadow

Aunt Teddy isn't with us long. It's not Mom's fault that she's gone. Just because Mom came home one night and yelled about her being there didn't mean Aunt Teddy had to move. But she did, the very next day. Maybe Teddy didn't understand that Mom gets cantankerous at times and the best thing to do, if that happens, is keep quiet and still. Not move out.

Still, after a week or maybe a month, she stops by. She checks on us. And whenever she's here, she teaches me the next line.

"Yea, though I walk." Aunt Teddy waits for me to repeat her words.

"Yea, though I walk," I say.

"Through the valley . . ."

"Through the valley . . ."

"Of the shadow of death."

"Wait. I don't want to walk there."

"No one does. But there's a reason to learn this," she promises.

I love Aunt Teddy, but I can only go so far.

"Through the valley of the shadow," I offer.

"Through the valley of the shadow of death," she prompts.

"I'm not walking that far. I'm just going to the valley of the shadow."

I should be too young to know of valleys and shadows, yet because I do know about them, I long for her to tell me again about green pastures and safe waters. I cling to the truths about a Shepherd who rescues, a Provider, and a Protector. I can't imagine what any of it really means and I don't even know if I *really* believe what she's telling me, but with everything in me, I want to believe.

Reality for the Kauffman kids is mostly defined by lack of rescue, absent providers, and negligent protection. Looking out for ourselves, we become adept at resourcefulness.

"Hey look, paint." Annie hops down from the kitchen counter one morning, where she's been rummaging for something to eat. In her hand is a tiny box with four bottles of bright liquid.

"Let's see." Lilly grabs it. "It's not paint. It's food coloring."

We gather in a knot to puzzle over the find.

"It's food?" I ask.

"No, it's for coloring food," Lilly says, studying the box.

"If I had food, I'd eat it not color it," John decides, walking away.

Lilly reads the back of the box as she follows him out, which leaves me and Annie face-to-face.

"What are you looking at?" she says.

The next day, we scoot our chairs around the table for our mush. Lilly carries the pot from the kitchen as usual, but with the first scoop, we see our world has changed. The mush is red.

The USDA government surplus commodity oatmeal tastes the same. But now, it also keeps us guessing. We don't know what Lilly might cook up: red mush one day, blue the next. When a steaming bowl of green mush is set before me, I think of green pastures.

Multicolored mush isn't our only surprise. A day comes when Dad announces we are moving.

"How come?" I ask.

Everyone is too busy throwing things in boxes and piling them into the backseat of the car to explain. The big kids are excited because we're leaving the Projects. Dad has bought a house, they say—a *house!*

"But what about Mom?"

"Shut up. Come help."

"But what about Aunt Teddy?"

"Put this blanket in that bag. Come on, we're going."

In the hubbub we learn the house is on Beacon Hill, and that sends everyone over the top because it's a name we recognize from our long walk to Teddy's.

"Beacon Avenue, remember?" We turn to each other.

"Remember? The ants go marching one by one, remember?"

We are too young to grasp the significance of the move from the Projects—the place where we had lived for one year and where the marriage of Johnnie and Josie fell apart. Of the handful of Seattle's housing projects for the poor in 1960, the one we were leaving carried the ironic name High Point. The older kids, who longed for the way things used to be back in Idaho, before we moved to the Projects, perhaps thought we were returning to some form of stability. That wasn't the case. We were simply changing locations. We did, however, get a new addition to the family.

"He's my dog," Annie decrees.

"No. He's all of ours," John dismisses. But when he walks away, Annie mouths the words, "My dog."

The big kids name him Shadow because a dark, almost black stripe runs down his back. John says he looks like a German Shepherd, but different. Lilly says he's like a husky, but different. Annie reasons the "different" must mean he's part coyote, since he came from the reservation. They mull that over for a while, petting Shadow's shadow, and finally agree that he must be part coyote. Listening to them, I wonder if we're part coyote too, since we came from the reservation like he did.

Shadow licks Lotta's face and knocks over Baby. He jumps up on Carla, on me, on Annie, and then flies up the steps of the house and dashes in and out of the bedrooms.

"Get him outside," Lilly yells.

The big kids tie him to a tree but he chews through the rope and zooms back into the house to tackle us.

"He's here to keep us safe," Lilly announces, forgiving Shadow for getting loose. "His barking will keep strangers away."

And he does protect us, by barking at everyone and everything, but we hardly do anything to protect him in return. Not once do we buy dog food, and there isn't much in the way of table scraps. In time, you can tell this dog is a Kauffman because his ribs show like ours.

Half-coyote reservation dogs know how to survive. Even though Dad buys a chain to replace the chewed-through rope, Shadow breaks free and wanders the city to hunt. He comes home with a mallard duck, limp between his jaws, and eats it. Another time, he returns with part of a deer, so big and heavy he keeps dropping it and dragging it. We speculate about where he found a deer in Seattle.

"Probably at the zoo, the Woodland Park zoo."

"No, stupid. They have cages at the zoo."

"Maybe he went to the mountains."

"Hey, maybe Shadow went back to Idaho for his deer!"

One day, he goes for fast food, bolting straight across the street into a corner grocery store, owned by an old Chinese couple. Racing so fast his paws slide on the linoleum, Shadow aims for the first food in sight—a display rack of potato chips. Nabbing a bag in his teeth, he whirls 180 degrees and claws his way out of the store. We watch from the porch as Shadow whizzes toward us like a missile. The elderly man and his wife chase after him, their white aprons flapping as they yell in Chinese. We don't know what they're saying but know it can't be good. Still, we cheer for Shadow as we open the front door for him. He flies past us, the torn bag of chips in his teeth. We slam the door behind him, whooping and hollering and grabbing up the chips that fall from the bag, sharing in Shadow's bounty.

# Chapter 9

"Hattie!" Jeanie's voice shot through the speakerphone of my car. "Do you have a Bible?"

"Um, there's one in the house, I think."

"Well, get it. Read Isaiah 54."

"Why?"

"Just read it. Isaiah 54."

She hung up.

At home that night, I scanned the shelves for a Bible, unsure if we still had one. Yes—there it was. The feel of the leather cover in my hands reminded me of the Bible Aunt Teddy had given me when I was a child.

*I wonder what became of it?*

I flipped the pages until I found Isaiah 54. In the middle were these words:

Fear not; for thou shalt not be ashamed: neither be thou confounded . . .

For thy Maker is thine husband; the Lord of hosts is his name . . .

For the Lord hath called thee as a woman forsaken and grieved in spirit. (vv. 4–6 KJV)

I read it again.

"Fear not . . . thy Maker is thine husband."

The metallic screech of the garage door rising on its tracks interrupted me. My husband was home. *No. "Thy Maker is thine husband."* Shaking my head at the coincidence of his arrival at that moment, I walked swiftly to my room, the Bible in hand, and shut and locked the door. God was my husband.

*What could that mean?*

Climbing into bed and turning off the light, I remembered the bedtime prayers Aunt Teddy taught me to pray—simple, childlike, and honest. When she visited us in our house on Beacon Hill, she had me memorize the books of the Bible. I'd stand before her, a second or third grader, and recite: "Genesis, Exodus, Leviticus, Numbers, Deuteronomy . . ." *How odd*, I thought, *that she'd wanted a little girl to memorize those names. What possible use could it have been?*

Teddy taught me other things that I actually did use, like how to plant flower bulbs in the ground and wait for them to bloom. Thinking about this lady who loved me, and loved God, I switched the light back on and looked over at the Bible on my nightstand, noticing I'd set it on top of an empty notebook a friend had given me. That gift was a subtle encouragement to "journal" my experience, which I had ignored. But the Bible on the notebook propelled me. I opened the journal to an empty page and wrote my first prayer: "Dear God . . ."

*What do I say to God?*

"Please take care of me."

Feeling self-conscious, I stopped there, wrestling with my memory of rejecting Teddy and her God. Had I believed the prayers I mouthed as a child, or was I just so desperate for an adult's attention that I parroted back to her whatever she wanted?

I remembered that when I was about nine or ten years old, the Twenty-Third Psalm had finally made sense to me. The "I shall not want" did not mean "the Lord is my Shepherd, the one I shall not want," but instead meant, "with the Lord as my Shepherd, I shall be satisfied, not left wanting anything." Yes, I had believed. I recalled that I used to pray, even when Teddy wasn't at our house with us. Looking down at the journal on my lap, and the scrawl, "Please take care of me," I realized the plea wasn't so different from the nighttime prayers I whispered as a child. Settling into a feeling of comfort, I turned out the light and went to sleep.

In the following days, my written prayers, though tentative, began to expand. "Dear God, I don't know what I am supposed to do next." "God, I feel . . . lost . . . I don't have footing for this."

In adulthood, my goal had been to live a "normal" life, and that, I thought, meant a stable home. I could overlook much for normalcy. Normalcy was more than a salve to the chaos of childhood. It counterbalanced the unpredictability of my career, which might find me covering a plane crash one day, a kidnapping the next, or a midnight call to do a live shot on a wildfire or flood. My "normal" home life, however, was devolving into something more intimate to me: heightened anxiety with an ever-present hint of harm.

## Divorce

"Divorce? I don't understand."

"What? What happened?"

"They're getting divorced."

"No, they *already* got divorced."

"Who got divorced?"

"Mom and Dad!"

"How come?"

"Never mind."

"What are you guys talking about?"

"Shush. Take the Kids outside."

"But . . . what happened? What's going on?"

Despite the divorce, our parents remain intertwined. Maybe that's why we don't notice it at first, because nothing really changes.

They're still in and out as erratically as before, sometimes with other people in tow.

Mom gets a skinny boyfriend named Howard. His jokes are so stupid, we call him Howie. Then he vanishes, and I think it's our fault for making fun of him.

Dad gets the Alaskan Woman, or at least, that's what we hear.

"You and that Alaskan Woman," Mom shouts. "Go to your Alaskan Woman." "Where's your Alaskan Woman now?"

Next, Mom is with the totem pole carver. He's as invisible as the Alaskan Woman, but his presence grows as we imagine towering evergreen trees chopped down for his workshop. Like a legend, he's someone who does great things somewhere else. Mom is with him. I picture her in a large hall with wood chips all over the floor, wearing her red shirt, with her black hair curling down past her shoulders as she watches the carver bent over a giant felled cedar, his features obscured as he chips away.

"What time is it?" Annie pulls me from my daydream.

"I don't know."

"Well, you better get going," she says, pouring coffee into a thermos of Dad's to take with her for lunch. "It's a school day."

"Oh. OK."

I begin the search for two shoes that match.

In the elementary school lunchroom, while other kids pull bologna sandwiches from their paper lunch bags, Annie, a third grader, will drink black coffee from her thermos.


## The Ride

"A latte, please. Skim, and can you make it half-caff?"

Jeanie and I were meeting for a late breakfast. I couldn't wait to talk about the Scripture she'd had me read. And yet, I worried whether my sudden appetite for ancient Bible verses was evidence of my own imbalance.

As usual, Jeanie was impeccable in Ralph Lauren, her hair perfectly highlighted, a designer handbag at her side, as she leisurely scanned the menu, deciding what to order.

My mind swirled with other questions. *What happens next? Does he take my savings? Do I end up broke, in addition to old and all alone?* I knew a woman who discovered her husband having an affair with their children's nanny, and in the divorce, she had to pay *him* alimony. Horror stories like that seemed to bombard me from every friend, colleague, co-worker, and acquaintance, feeding my fear. Is that why I'd responded so strongly to a bunch of words promising me a husband who would not abandon or forsake me? Or was there more to it?

"The veggie omelet," she said finally. "Egg white only."

I couldn't think about food.

"Yogurt and fruit," I said quickly just to get rid of the waiter. And then, I launched in.

"I read Isaiah 54, in fact, I keep reading it. I can't stop."

"Isn't it great? I thought of you as soon as I saw it."

"Did you know there are all sorts of translations?" I asked. "Some Bibles are older English. But some are right now, current English. They word it: 'The LORD will call you back as if you were a wife deserted and distressed in spirit.' It blows me away. Every time I read it, it's like God is talking right to me. I know that's crazy."

"Why do you say it's crazy?"

"Well . . ."

"Listen, don't doubt yourself. And don't doubt God."

I leaned toward Jeanie, hoping she'd take the hint to lower her voice. Though eager to learn more, I was embarrassed to be talking about God so openly. I was a news correspondent, after all. And here we were in a twenty-first-century, wi-fi equipped, power lunch spot, surrounded by—I glanced at the other tables—plenty of evidence of plastic surgery, but no Bibles.

"The minute I read it, I knew it was for you. And hasn't it been helpful?" she asked.

"Yes." I sat quietly for just a second, considering how she may have happened upon that verse. "Do you read the Bible often?"

"Yes. And I pray."

We'd been friends a decade, but this was new territory. I felt that something larger than either of us was at work, and I no longer cared if other diners overheard us.

"You pray?" I asked.

"Every day."

"I didn't know that."

"I have a prayer closet."

*A closet?*

"Read Matthew 6:6 and you'll understand," she said.

I felt dumbstruck that we were speaking in code: Matthew 6:6, after Isaiah 54. On the sidewalk outside the window, several women passed by, Rodeo Drive shopping bags swinging from their wrists. They were like reminders of another world, one I used to inhabit, alien from where I now sat pondering a prayer closet.

The word *prayer* brought to mind the heavyset black woman I'd interviewed the day after learning my marriage was over, the one who had embraced me and declared, "Women all over the world will be praying for you." I had thought she was nuts. Was that only a couple months ago? It was astounding how much had changed in so little time. Now, my own prayers were written in a journal by my bedside, and here was Jeanie informing me of her prayer closet.

I gazed back at my friend as if seeing her for the first time. She was in midsentence, describing a fabulous little shop down the street that had the best kids' clothes, and did I want to go with her to shop for the grandkids? Yes, I nodded, smiling wide at Jeanie's effortless bridging of two worlds: shopping and prayer.

The entwining of those words brought one more memory of the woman I'd interviewed. She had said God told her to sell products made by women in Africa. We, a network news crew, were there to do a story about successful home businesses. Yet the one point she was adamant about, that *God* told her to start the business, was the very statement that ended up on the cutting room floor. I had included it in the original news script, not because I believed it, but because the woman had said it. The producer, however, insisted it be dropped.

"We can't put that in there. People will think she's crazy, 'hearing voices from God.'"

As the producer rolled her eyes, I shrugged my shoulders, letting it go—and so the very essence of the woman's story never made it on the air.

Trying to return my attention to Jeanie, I had the nagging thought that now I occupied the place of the woman I'd interviewed: the place of "She's crazy. She believes in God." Although I hadn't actually made a declaration of belief, I was scribbling prayers on paper and reading Isaiah 54 and hadn't considered, until just that moment, how precarious it might be to actually follow God in a world where people think you're insane for doing so.

And what else had she said to me? I scanned my memory searching for her words. That was it. She'd said, "I couldn't ignore God," even though she had no idea how to proceed. I was beginning to feel the same way. It was like I'd stepped onto a ride that was equal parts exhilarating and terrifying, because I clearly wasn't in control of the ride and didn't know if I could get off if I wanted to.

## No Seat Belts

"Look out!"

The car lurches to the left as Dad peels Mom's hands off the steering wheel. While they fight for control of the car, we in the backseat flop against each other, to the right, to the left.

"Stop!" Lilly cries.

Dad accelerates. Mom's fists pummel his head.

"Whoa!" Annie yells as we almost hit a light pole.

"That's no totem pole," Dad sneers.

Mom turns to open the passenger door, threatening to jump.

"No, Mom, no," we scream, almost as one.

Dad reaches over to grip her elbow and yank her toward him. Left free, the passenger door swings wildly open. We turn a corner and it slams shut with a bang. For a second we're relieved.

But then, uh-oh, we know what's ahead. We know where we are. On the back side of Beacon Hill is McClellan Street; a hill so steep it's cut into four sections like steps down the incline.

"Hold on." John grabs for Baby.

Our heads bump the top of the car as we descend over the edge. Momentarily airborne, our tummies tickle. Then, *whap*, we're back on the road.

"Whoa!"

Instantly we're lifted back into the air as the car flies into the next drop. It would be fun . . .

"Whee!"

. . . except Mom might jump.

"Dad, stop!"

Lotta is crying.

"Whoa!"

Carla starts crying too. She, like Lotta, has already had a broken bone. Carla's happened when her nose hit the dashboard back when we lived in the Projects.

Airborne over the next drop of the hill, I close my eyes, and think to myself the words Aunt Teddy taught me.

"I shall fear no evil," she says.

"I shall fear no evil," I repeat.

"For Thou art with me."

"For Thou art with me."

# Chapter 10

Jeanie was unwavering, as we sat once again in her living room. My unofficial therapist, she told me to make a list of his betrayals and tape it on my bedroom door to remind myself not to talk to him.

"Look at what he's done," she said. "He lied to you, plotted against you, rifled through your documents, consulted lawyers before he let you know there was a problem. He told your *friends* he was going to divorce you! Hattie, these are not the actions of a kind person."

"Maybe he's just having a midlife crisis and . . ."

I stopped talking when I saw the revulsion on her face. I wasn't sure why I was still trying to excuse him. It embarrassed me.

"Hattie, there are grown-up ways of asking for a divorce. There's a decent, adult way of saying 'I'm not happy about it, but I need to do this. It's not you. It's me. I'm the problem, and I'm terribly sorry for the pain I'm causing.' Did he say anything like that?"

I shook my head.

"Has he even said the words 'I'm sorry'?"

Again, I shook my head.

"No," Jeanie continued. "Instead, he says hurtful things like 'I just settled for you.' He blamed *you*. Listen, you've done nothing to deserve this treatment."

Emboldened by Jeanie, I began to build a wall of separation around me. Granted, it wasn't built with bricks; it was more of a miniature Lego block wall. But it was a start.

When I got home, I saw he'd left grocery store coupons on the counter for me, as if I were still doing the family shopping. Throwing them out, I said, "Wives clip coupons. I'm not a wife anymore."

I stopped paying for the maid who came every week. If he wanted a clean house he could pay for it. Looking at the satellite TV bill, I asked myself, *Which one of us is sitting out there watching the big screen?* It wasn't me. So I quit paying the bill.

## Cold House

We are used to things being shut off, one by one. The gas is first. We understand it has to do with bills not being paid. But that's the world of adults. For us kids, it means that one day the furnace doesn't rumble on like it used to, and all at once we're cold. My brother, sisters, and I find blankets or sheets, or even towels, to wrap around our shoulders. Walking about the frigid house in our coverings, we look like tiny Hollywood movie Indians in their blankets around the campfire. Our fire is a small electric heater in the living room that glows red. By day, we stand in a ring around it. At night, we drag the mattress down to sleep by it.

It doesn't take long to learn that with the gas shut off, there's no hot water.

Annie, the coffee drinker, comes up with a plan. We can heat water, she explains, by plugging in the tall, aluminum, electric percolator.

"Just don't put coffee in it," she says, as she demonstrates.

We can even take baths, if we make a dozen trips from the

kitchen, carefully carrying the percolator by its two little black handles, upstairs to the bathroom, dump the water into the tub, return to the kitchen to fill up the percolator again, plug it in, and wait for it to heat. By the time we haul the next pot up, the water in the tub is cool, so cool that the whole thing would seem pointless except we figure out that if you jump in immediately after the last pot, and if you aim your butt exactly where it was poured, well, it's not too bad. Annie gets the first bath.

"How come you always get the warm water?"

"Because I made it possible, now get out of here."

We take turns. One washes, and then another jumps in. Baby is last every time but she's too young to complain. We are all a year older than we were at the Projects, and we know a lot more, but Baby is still too young to complain.

A few weeks after the gas is shut off, something worse happens. The electricity goes out. It happens when it's daylight, so the first thing we notice is the silence. There's no refrigerator noise, no fan, nothing; only quiet. When sundown comes, silence isn't the problem. No matter how many times we flick the light switches, we are caught in a dark so absolute we need to reach out to find each other. Frightened, we learn to run to the bathroom to pee before the blackness of night arrives. In the dark, each creak and groan of the old house sounds sinister. Oddly, we become terrified of the basement door, as if the blackness down there is more threatening than the darkness right here. Gathered on the mattress on the living room floor, next to the heater whose coils no longer glow, we miss the red light of our campfire even more than we miss its heat. We let Shadow in, so we can snuggle next to his fur.

"I'm scared."

"Shhh, go to sleep."

"I'm scared."

"What was that?"

"Nothing. Go to sleep."

"Stop pushing."

"Scoot over."

"I'm scared."

"I'm cold."

"Did you hear something?"

"Shush, go to sleep."

With blankets piled over us, we drop into whispers, like our regular voices lost power because a grown-up didn't pay the bill. The little ones cling to the oldest. To calm them, John and Lilly tell stories about our old life in Idaho.

"We always had food," Lilly remembers. "We had a cow for milk, and chickens for eggs."

"Milk anytime you wanted?" I ask.

"Yep."

"We had a peach tree," John adds. "And a cherry tree, and an apple tree."

"Walnut tree too," Annie says.

I think she's making that up, but I don't say it.

"Remember when Dad used to give us a penny for each potato bug we picked off the potato plants?" John's whisper sounds like it's smiling.

"I want a potato. I'm hungry."

"Shh . . ."

"Walnuts don't grow on trees."

"Yes, they do."

"I want a walnut."

"Shush."

They go on about the tiny farm, the cow named Bobby, and the horse named Lady. They describe the pigpen and the chicken coop, the orchard and the vegetable garden, talking until there's nothing left to say about it all, except to ask why we left. But none of us ever asks, because no one wants to bring up Mom and Dad, and where they might be, or when they might come home. Eventually, we fall asleep, lying so close together that an arm is over someone's belly, a leg is in a side, an elbow on a nose, one head of hair tangled with the next. The luckiest are the ones in the middle. The unluckiest, on either outside edge, might wake up on the wooden floor, shivering in the pitch dark.

Despite the terror of the night, life goes on. We wake in a bundle and immediately fall into playing, fighting, or both. A favorite is the Shoe War. We run around stockpiling shoes for weapons. When the war begins, we fling them at each other. Getting hit by a shoe is supposed to mean you're dead, but we forget that we're killed or else we cheat and get back up to raid each other's stockpiles, so the War goes on.

Some days we go to school, when we remember to go and can find a pair of shoes that match. Often we're late, not only because it takes a while to find a matching shoe, especially after a Shoe War, but because without electricity, the kitchen clock doesn't work. And no one believes the cuckoo clock. So we go to school when we guess we should.

Baths are out of the question now that we can't make hot water with the electric coffee percolator. We take quick, cold, sponge baths at the sink, so quick that we're not exactly clean.

One morning, even that doesn't work. I turn the faucet, and nothing happens. I stare in wonder at the dry bathroom sink, as my hand turns the rusty faucet back and forth.

"Hey, it's broken. The bathroom sink is broken," I announce.

"Let me see."

"Get out of the way."

The bigger ones push me aside.

"The water must be shut off."

"It can't be. Pipes are like rivers. They flow forever."

For a second, the dry faucet leaves us mute.

"Let's check the kitchen," John says, and everybody trots downstairs.

That faucet is dry too.

"Proves it," he says. "The water company shut off service."

A general sorrow descends upon us. Every now and then, one or another tries the faucet again, just to make sure.

"What's a water company?" I ask. No one answers.

Our bathroom begins to stink. We shut the door to keep the odor inside. When we have to use the toilet, we take a big breath, race in, go, and then run out, slamming the door behind us. But the smell seeps into the hallway.

John and Lilly get the idea of walking to the gas station with an empty bucket, filling it with water and hauling it back to the house. The first bucket is always for flushing the toilet. The second bucket is drinking water.

Over the days, they take turns getting water. Then it's Annie's turn. And now, mine.

I want to protest that though only six blocks away, the gas station feels like it would be too long a walk for a first grader. But it's my turn, so I step out the front door swinging the bucket. I cross the street where the Chinese store is, and wonder if they got over the potato chips Shadow stole. Passing block after block, I begin the Ants Go Marching song, but it's not so fun all alone. I keep thinking I'm just the one ant. Instead, under my breath, I repeat, "Yea, though I walk . . . Yea, though I walk . . ." as I walk along, but stop when I remember the next line: "through the valley of the shadow of death." To distract myself from that scary thought, I try to recall whether we passed these houses the time we took the wrong bus, but none of them look familiar.

At last, I see the gas station ahead, yet instead of speeding up, I slow down, afraid someone might shout, "Hey Kid, you have to pay for that water!" I linger by the alley, looking at the gas station.

My favorite gas stations are the ones with the red flying horse. I want to ride a horse.

*I never got to ride Lady, the horse in Idaho. I wonder how come they called her Lady. I wonder where Aunt Teddy is. I wonder . . .*

I begin to swing the bucket back and forth. I'll get in trouble if I come back empty.

To stop staring at the gas station, I give myself a count. One, two, three . . . I gallop forward, the empty bucket flying wildly in my hand. When I reach the gas station I drop the bucket and grab the hose, squeezing the handle, which causes the water to spurt with such force the bucket quickly overflows. I drop the hose and grasp the bucket handle, expecting to race away, but the weight of the pail keeps me in place. It takes both hands, and tiny steps, to stagger away from the gas station.

I spill water as it sloshes from side to side. My legs and feet are soaked. The metal handle hurts my fingers. After every five or six steps, I need to rest.

When I'm almost home, a girl from my class pops out the door of a big white house.

"Hattie, what are you doing with that water?"

"Oh," I answer, and look at the bucket as if surprised to find it in my red raw hand. "Um, I was just getting ready to . . ."

I look around for an escape.

". . . ready to wash the car."

"Where's your car?" she asks.

"Over there."

I gesture with my chin to a car parked up the street.

"Your parents let you wash the car?" She seems impressed.

"Yep." I set the bucket down.

"Do you live here?" I ask to change the subject.

"No, just visiting my cousin," she says. "Where do you live?"

"Oh. Over there." I gesture again in the direction of the car that's supposed to be mine. She doesn't ask why I have a bucket so far from my house and car.

"Well, bye," I say.

"Bye." She skips back inside.

I slosh on home, to pour my bucket of water into the clogged and stinky toilet.

# Chapter 11

I rose early and tiptoed past his closed door, awkwardly carrying an overnight bag along with my purse and laptop. I wanted to get out the door to go to work without running into him, and would have been successful but for the noise of the garage door.

Suddenly, there he was behind me in his new "single guy" clothes. "How are you?" he squeaked.

*How am I?*

It was the first time he'd asked that in the two months since our divorce dinner. My mind could not form an answer, not for him, or even for myself. Half the time, I didn't know how I felt. The disintegration of what I thought was stability-in-marriage had me roiling in childhood memories of instability and abandonment. Why wasn't I recalling anything happy? Mom and Dad weren't always gone. Most days Dad came home from work and read the paper while Mom cooked dinner, like any other American couple. They bought us bikes one year and we went zooming around the neighborhood like normal children do. But the gash in my adult sense of normalcy had me dredging up only terrors. Summoning what it would take to tackle an explanation of "how I am" was not what I wanted to do for him. I couldn't even do it for myself.

So I waved weakly, dismissively, got in the car, and backed out of the garage.

*I need another way to exit the house.*

The next day I rose before dawn, dressed without turning on a light, and waited for the furnace to rumble on so it would muffle the "beep beep" of the alarm system and the noisy garage door. Standing in the dark, listening to the first birds wake, I felt poised for action; under duress but fortified for it. When the furnace kicked on, I moved quickly, punching in the code to disable the alarm, cracking open the French doors of my bedroom and stepping onto the darkened patio. I was like a prowler, except I was trying to break out rather than in.

I slipped around the side of the house and crept along the narrow path between our home and the neighbor's. In pre-planning the escape, I'd made a spare key to open the side gate, but hadn't considered that it would be too dark to see the lock. My shaky fingers felt for it, located it, and wrestled to turn the key. The warped gate needed a shove, but finally swung open to the front lawn. I sprinted across the grass, hoping he wouldn't catch my silhouette against the window of the guest room. Ducking onto the porch, I punched a code into a control panel near the front door to slide open the wrought iron gate at the driveway. Finally, taking a deep breath, I pushed the button on the handheld garage door opener.

The scraping, cranking noise of the door broke the predawn silence. I stooped to get under the still-rising door and jumped into my car. The engine seemed to roar when I turned the ignition. Quickly putting the car into reverse, I backed out before the garage door was fully open.

*Escape.*

I did this every morning to avoid bumping into him. But one evening we encountered each other, when he came in without my hearing him.

"I notice you've been leaving early," he said, walking toward me. "I'm sorry you feel you have to do that."

"Well, you could move out," I answered.

"I'm not moving."

He continued advancing. I took a few steps backward.

"Let's take it up in mediation," he said.

"You want to *mediate* moving out?" I asked, planting my feet. "What, you want me to pay you to move out? Is that it?"

He began to backpedal. It was my turn to walk forward.

"Will the mediator decide *I'm* the one to move out? Is that what you're after?"

I felt utter revulsion.

"Leave!" I yelled and flung open the front door to make his path out more clear. There was no response, not the flicker of a muscle, as cold air rushed in between us. Inexplicably, I recalled the exact words he spoke when he proposed. To spit out that memory, I shouted, "Get your skinny butt out of here, so I don't have to look at it."

It wasn't a very mighty thing to say. In my desperation to blurt out something to cut him to the core all I could muster was some lousy comment about his rump. Couldn't I have done better? Attacked his character? Called out his duplicity? Nope, I'd taken a swipe at his flat backside. To top it off, I was so irrational that, after shutting myself back in my room I felt sorry for my cheap shot.

*You're not supposed to call names.*

Immediately and impulsively, I went back to apologize, but he was no longer in the living room, so I tapped on his door.

"It's me. I'm sorry . . . that I said you, you know, that you have a skinny, uh . . . butt."

"Forget it," came the voice on the other side of the door.

"No, it's not right to call names. It's not nice. I'm sorry I said you have a skinny butt."

"Go to sleep!" he ordered.

Shuffling wretchedly back to my room, I felt embarrassed by my emotional outburst. Completely depleted, I didn't recognize the ridiculousness of my apology but had just enough sense to know there could be no more encounters. Not one. I checked the calendar.

*From this day forward, I will not see him nor speak to him.*

Resolved, I climbed into bed, reminding myself of Isaiah 54. *God is my husband.* With a deep sigh of exhaustion, I reclined back on the pillow, and that's when I wondered if God had a sense of humor. *He must.* I smiled, realizing that my vow meant the last words the man in the other room would hear from me were, "I'm sorry I said you have a skinny butt."

Tickled at myself, I tried to stifle the sound of my giggling by pulling the blankets overhead, but the hilarity of my apologizing was too much. I laughed out loud at myself, at my stupid outburst and at my stupendously stupid apology. I laughed at human beings, at men and women in general. Most of all, I laughed at my final two words.

## You Got the Butt

Buzzing in excitement, we're practically giggling as we set the table. Mom is home, cooking meat. Dad is here too, which makes it a family dinner, something so precious we almost tiptoe in anticipation.

When a family dinner goes well, we chatter over each other, laugh, and figure out how to divide one chicken among nine people. Someone always gets stuck with the heart or the gizzard. Someone else gets the neck. Whoever ends up with the back has to pick apart the chicken ribs. It doesn't matter. Everyone is happy, even as we tease each other.

"You got the butt."

"I did not."

"You did too. Look at that little piece right there. That's the chicken's butt."

"I don't want it. Trade you for the gizzard?"

But this night, our fragile dinner breaks apart like Humpty Dumpty. The meat Mom is making is called chipped beef on toast. We squirm as we take our seats for dinner, intoxicated with the aroma of it. But just as Dad is dishing out the stringy meat gravy onto his toast, he says something bad.

"In the army, we used to call this 's—t on a shingle.'"

Mom's five foot height doubles, or maybe that's us sinking into our chairs.

Her arm moves before we can duck. She grabs the nearest object, a bowl of canned peas, and slings it at him. Small, pale green orbs fly through the air and splatter upon him, the table, the walls, and us.

After the crash, there is not a sound. We kids freeze like statues, staring straight ahead, careful not to look toward Dad or Mom. If the goal is to avoid eye contact, I fail. Carla is directly across the table from me and catching her glance, I'm surprised to see a bit of mirth there. What could she possibly be happy about? The corners of her lips turn up. I take in the rest of her face and notice a mushy pea stuck to her forehead just above her eyelid, and two stuck to her cheek. Seeing them makes me conscious of my own face. A pea is slowly sliding down to the tip of my nose. Looking at it makes me cross-eyed, which causes Carla to struggle in an effort not to laugh. I meet her brave twinkle with one of my own. In merriment, we keep our bodies still as our eyes examine each other's pea-stricken faces.

The rest of the fight, the profanity, name-calling, and slamming of doors is eclipsed by the effort of my sister and me trying not to laugh aloud—our secret joy revealed only in our eyes.

# Chapter 12

"Look at her dress," Annie sneers, one afternoon when we're outside peering at the girl we've decided we all hate.

Candy walks past in her pretty dress, which gathers at the waist. We despise her for her dresses and her shiny black shoes with the dainty strap across the top.

"She's an only child," Lilly mutters.

"What?" I ask, mystified anyone could be without brothers or sisters.

"Well then, she's the only, only child in the Projects," Annie whispers.

"Only, only?"

"Shut up." I get an elbow.

Candy has blonde hair and a mom and dad who never come home drunk. She has toys.

"And look. Candy has candy."

I want to point out how funny that sounds, "Listen guys: The only, only Candy has candy!" But not wanting to get elbowed again, I keep my mouth shut.

We peer at Candy and plan attacks on her. Everyone does. The Gonzales family, with its seven kids, and the Marks family's fourteen kids, all watch Candy with fascination and envy. Some days, one kid or another will run up and smack her. She never hits back but just opens her mouth in a helpless wail. That's when the attacker turns tail to hide before Candy's mom or dad races out of their unit. They ask her what happened, but she only sobs and points down the sidewalk. Sometimes, her mom or dad will stalk the street, looking for the culprit, but usually they carry her inside while giving the empty yards dirty looks.

On this day, Candy eats her candy on her porch, too close to her front door for an attack. We watch until we're bored. Then, we wander to other parts of the neighborhood.

It is a warm afternoon some weeks later when I get caught in the aftermath of an attack.

"Run!" warns a kid flying past me.

"Candy's dad's coming," another yells.

I turn on my heels but our front door is too far. I'll never make it. Just ahead is the parking lot. I run for it and fall to the ground.

"Dang kids," a man's voice pounds.

I roll over until I'm hidden between two parked cars, listening for his footsteps, imagining him finding me. I hadn't hit Candy. It wasn't me. He won't believe me. I press myself flat on the pavement and inch my way under one of the cars.

The underside of the engine is above me. I hold my breath. A man's shoe appears to the left; another step, another shoe. I keep still, the rough metal guts of the car inches above my face.

*Don't find me.*

The shoes move on.

I stay in my hiding spot for a long time, fearing his return. The thought that someone might come along and start the car finally makes me move.

I don't know who hit Candy that time.

On a different day, Carla gets the blame.

Our kitchen door flies open and there's Candy's mom yanking a crying Carla in one hand and a crying Candy in the other; a threesome I never thought I'd see. More amazing, Candy's mom walks right in, like she lives here.

"Your kid hits my kid?" she demands. "Well, my kid's hitting back!"

She grabs a long-handled serving spoon off the counter. It's our spoon, in our kitchen.

"Here," she tells Candy. "Take it. Hit her."

Candy just sobs.

"Take it!" Her mom jerks Candy forward and presses the spoon into her hand. "Hit her."

Carla turns to us for help, her eyes huge.

But we can't do anything. We're as incapable as Candy.

"I said hit her," the mom yells.

She forces her daughter's hand up and uses the girl's arm as a weapon, smashing the spoon down on Carla's face. Again. And again.

Carla howls. That gets all of us crying, me, Lotta, Baby, even Annie, who is the Boss this day.

I want somewhere to hide, but can't think where. I need a base. Like playing tag, you know you're safe when you're on base.

"You can't get me. I'm on base!"

But with Candy's mom hitting our sister, in our own house, I can't imagine where a safe base would be.

## Dress the Part

My resolve to have no encounters with him meant I had to transform the master bedroom into a self-contained sanctuary, my safe base. I bought a mini-refrigerator and set it up on the bathroom counter, right next to a drip coffeemaker that I purchased to make hot water for tea or cup-of-soup.

I dragged in coats and purses from the hall closet, extra towels from the linen closet, books and photo albums from the home office.

With stacks of stuff lining the walls of the bedroom, it looked like my life was shrinking. I was setting up a homeless shelter inside a home.

It would take fortitude to get through this.

He giveth power to the faint; and to them that have no might he increaseth strength. (Isa. 40:29 KJV)

After reading Isaiah 54 countless times, I decided to read all of Isaiah, making notes in my journal when something jumped out at me.

"He giveth power to the faint."

The words themselves gave me strength. Bible reading remained my secret. Aside from Jeanie, my women friends seemed to be atheist, Jewish, Buddhist, or some New Age Hindu Yoga stew. When learning of my crumbling marriage, one suggested I chant "nam myoho renge kyo," and for a couple days I actually did, though only when stuck in traffic. Another friend offered the I-ching sticks. Most, however, simply gave me phone numbers for their divorce lawyers.

"Remember, divorce is adversarial," warned Drea. "Don't try to be his friend."

One woman advised having an affair immediately, before time ran out and we reconciled.

She, and others, meant well, even while missing the mark.

"Oh Hattie, I heard the news," declared teary-eyed Karen, a widow in perpetual mourning for a husband dead five years. She pulled me into a tight hug, releasing me long enough to look sadly into my eyes while declaring, "Divorce is *worse* than having your husband die, because it means he *wanted* to leave."

Another, whose husband had left her a decade earlier, sinking her into a puddle of woe from which she still hadn't emerged, seemed almost eager at my news, as if it meant she would have company in her dark pit. I recoiled at the prospect and felt guilty for avoiding her leaden calls.

Another took the opposite approach: lighthearted "retail therapy."

"Spend a lot of money," she advised. "Nothing beats an expensive dress."

## A Dress?

A dress, a dress, where's a dress?

I leap across the mattress on the floor, scramble through the tangled blankets, make my way past a shoe fort. I can't find a dress in any of the clothes piled everywhere.

"Just a minute," I yell down to Aunt Teddy.

I was in panties and an undershirt when I answered the door. Everyone was asleep but me. And there was Aunt Teddy on the porch, saying, "Do you want to see what Sunday school is like? Do you want to go to church with me?"

I can't find a dress. I can't find two shoes. There are no socks. I stand in the room where my sisters sleep. In the corner, I spy one of the T-shirts that Mom and Dad brought back for us when they went to San Francisco to get married again. We each got a T-shirt with our name on it, embroidered in loopy cursive letters that we had marveled at. I pick up the shirt, hoping it says "Hattie," but it says "Carlotta" in bright green stitching.

"Hattie?" Teddy calls from the bottom of the stairs.

"Don't leave!"

I am starting to cry, running down the steps with the Carlotta T-shirt in my hand.

"Don't leave."

"Oh, dear." Teddy hugs me. "Oh, dear . . ." After a few minutes, she says, "Let's find you a dress."

She finds something, and even irons it. I sit on the floor, hugging my bare knees. I don't want Teddy to leave, ever. But she is going away from us, she says, to be a missionary.

"What's that?"

"Do you remember 'The Lord is my shepherd'?" she asks.

"Yes."

"I'm going to teach other people about the Lord, and how he can be their shepherd. In Guatemala."

Since I don't know where that is, it's like hearing her say "I'm going across the street" or "I'm going to the store." In my ignorance, I nod while she talks, more interested in the transformation of my wrinkled old dress than in what she's saying, just as we were more impressed with the lettered T-shirts than with the fact that Mom and Dad got married again. I admire the crispness of the cloth as she slides the ironed dress over my head. Holding hands we hop down the steps to her car. This dress, I think, shows the world that someone cares about me, and that makes me valuable. I will spend much of my life disbelieving that the girl under the dress is valuable just for who she is.

By the third grade, I long for Aunt Teddy and am more aware than ever how different I am from the other kids at school.

The door to the portable classroom slams shut behind me. Startled students glance up from their work; I'm late as usual. Normally, I would ignore them and walk to my seat, but this day Mrs. Huntington, our teacher, stops me with her look. Her face says something's wrong.

"Children, keep reading," she tells the class, as she rushes toward me. Before I can take a step into the room, she has her hand on my shoulder, steering me back outside.

I must be in trouble. I wonder if she's taking me to the principal's office. Sure, I was late, but that's nothing new, so why am I in trouble? Once we're in the main building, she turns me toward the lavatory.

It is a long narrow room with open toilet stalls on the left and a rectangular enamel sink against the opposite wall. She marches me to the sink and runs the water. I don't understand what's happening because she hasn't explained and I'm too afraid to ask.

Mrs. Huntington cranks on the paper towel wheel and tears off a big piece. She holds it under the water, crinkles it in her fist, and begins scrubbing my face with it. I wince at the harshness of the paper against my skin. Gradually, I feel ashamed at how dirty I must be if my teacher has to wash me so hard.

Next, she pulls a comb from her pocket and tries to run it through my hair, stinging my scalp as the tangles snag the comb. I don't cry or complain. She yanks to the left, then to the right, and finally gives up. Our eyes meet briefly in the mirror, while she considers my mane. I dart my eyes away and hear Mrs. Huntington sigh. She puts the comb back in her pocket. For an instant, we do nothing. Abruptly, she turns on the water again, cups her hands under the faucet, and spills a little puddle on top of my head. While rivulets roll down my face, she pats my wet hair, pushing it behind my ears, smoothing it all around. It takes several cupped handfuls before she gets it slicked back, and somewhat tamed.

Finally, she tugs on my sleeves, straightening my dress. She spins me around and puts the buttons in the buttonholes all the way up the back. She swivels me to face the mirror again, and nods at what she sees. I'm embarrassed by the attention, yet feel a glimmer of love for Mrs. Huntington. She is taking care of me.

Not a word has been spoken, but as we walk back to the portable, she peeks down and gives me a tiny grin. I beam a smile back at her.

# Chapter 13

Living as a refugee became routine. My lawyer had basically ordered me not to vacate the house—to do so would imply surrender of the home, she said. Regaining possession would be nearly impossible. But living, or rather concealing, myself under the same roof for more than a few days was unbearable.

At night, I stayed at Jeanie's, where I had my own bedroom with white linens. In her library, I found an old Bible that she said once belonged to her mother. I loved flipping through the thin pages and finding verses that were long ago underlined.

> But, O Lord of hosts, that triest the righteous, and seest the reins and the heart, let me see thy vengeance on them: for unto thee have I opened my cause. (Jer. 20:12 KJV)

I couldn't help but wonder what might have been happening in the woman's life when she highlighted the passages.

> Consider the work of God: for who can make that straight, which he hath made crooked? (Eccles. 7:13 KJV)

My life was crooked and it was tempting to latch on to Jeanie's hospitality in an attempt to straighten it. I longed to nest there but I feared overstaying my welcome, so I limited my stay at Jeanie's to two-night stints. Other nights, I slept on the lumpy couch of an artist friend, with her Shiva statues and good luck bamboo sprouts pushed aside to make room for me. Often, my refuge was an out-of-town work assignment, since I volunteered for anything that might take me away.

"We'd be honored, Ms. Kauffman, if you could give the keynote at our conference . . ." I was occasionally asked to speak, and in my married life often declined so that I wouldn't be on the road any more than my job already required. But now, on the road was exactly where I needed to be. I scanned the email to see where the conference was. Anchorage, Alaska. Bingo.

"I would be happy to give your keynote . . ." I typed.

After the speech, I hopped on a day cruise of Prince William Sound. The snap of cold air enlivened me as I stood on deck, bracing myself against the wind while we glided past seemingly untouched wilderness. After a time, I noticed that some of the tourists on board wore matching name tags. What caught my eye was the tiny cross in the corner of each tag. Curious, I began to trail them about the ship, in a shy way, hanging back a few steps, uncertain why they interested me. Finally, I asked a lady how I could find out more about their group and she pointed to a man and said, "Talk to the pastor."

He seemed to have a gaggle of people about him every time I tried to approach and so, feeling increasingly ridiculous, I hung about the edge as they went from top deck to dining room to gift shop. At last, space suddenly opened up in front of the pastor and I plunged in before I could think what to say.

"Your name tags with crosses . . . Uh, do people who believe in God take vacations together?"

A couple of women chuckled and I heard one say, "We've got a live one here."

Feeling my face flush, I nodded as he told me they were from a church in Wisconsin, my feet already inching backward in embarrassment.

Flying home, I had a moment of quiet laughter at my stalking of Christians on a cruise. Obviously it was the *group* aspect of their trip that had enthralled me, I thought. Kicked to the curb in my married life, I must have been unconsciously drawn to the sense of belonging they evoked; the group embrace, the warm huddle. That reasoning pushed my smile away. I knew I was flying back to a place where I no longer knew how to belong.

On the days when I didn't have somewhere to go—like Jeanie's, or a work assignment—I drove around LA until it was very late. Hoping he was asleep, I crept back into the house, retracing the escape route, to gain entry, quietly, furtively. Weekends were the worst. Without the office as a haven, I drove hundreds of miles around Southern California, through sunrises and sunsets, past neon city lights, or through dark, curving canyons, occasionally tearful but more often just baffled and empty.

Sometimes it seemed my grief was due to the loss of my role rather than the loss of another's love. I liked being a wife: the cooking, the caretaking, the checking in. But intermittently, on these long winding drives, I experienced a wild excitement, an exuberance at the prospect of being free.

During one such drive that thought cut me to the quick, revealing a part of my married life I hadn't wanted to examine. Over the years, I had kept myself busy, preoccupied in my job and often out of town. It was a career that accommodated an unexamined marriage. Annoyances at home could be endured because I wasn't there consistently. Yes, the electric guitar signed by a rock star that he hung in the entryway was a bit much, but I'd get used to it, and if I couldn't, well, I took trips to my cabin. Alone.

*Hattie. You would go to Montana for a month at a time. Without him. Regularly.*

I wrestled with the dawning sense that I had, for a long time, felt squelched, and began to see the contortions I'd gone through to deny that feeling. I had averted my eyes until there were so many

106

signed guitars hanging all over the house it looked like we lived in a Hard Rock Café.

Dumbfounded at these realizations, I pulled the car to the curb, finding it impossible to drive while admitting that no one had been at the wheel for . . . how long?

I remembered the day almost a year ago when he'd picked up the TV remote and switched from the morning program I reported for to another, and announced we would watch *that* one from now on. I hadn't objected. Incredibly, I instead had zeroed in on the TV screen rather than on what was happening between the two of us. With a misplaced focus, I noticed the competing morning show had brighter color graphics than my show. At work that day, I told one of my producers that the other network had brighter onscreen graphics, and perhaps we should let New York know.

*What had happened to me?*

Weary with disbelief at the extent of my denial, I bent my head down to my chest and cried for myself, for all that I had been living with—for the avoiding, explaining, and swallowing. But the sorrow was brief and quickly overtaken by a dazzling desire to shout, "Thank you for setting me free!"—though I wasn't sure who to address that to. The thought of gratitude toward him didn't seem right, and yet gratitude was due somewhere.

Looking up, I saw I had pulled over near a beach. I got out of the car, kicked off my shoes, and walked onto the sand, surprised at its warmth underfoot. The wind had shifted, as it can in Southern California, sending a summer day in midwinter. I sat and stared at the water, my mind quiet after so many somersaults. Eventually, I lay back; the sand conformed to my body like a hug, and in its embrace I relaxed into a doze.

Male voices snapped me out of sleep. Disoriented, I sat up and saw to my left a group of teenage boys walking toward me on the darkened shore. Their eyes and attention were locked on me.

I scrambled up and hurried away as quickly as feet slipping in sand would allow. Once safely locked in my car, an old sensation stirred me and felt oddly welcome: adrenaline. I felt alive and tough. No, of course I shouldn't have been alone on the beach after sunset, but I had sensed danger and fled—meaning my survival instincts still worked. I'd forgotten this part of me, yet how could I? I chuckled to myself. *I grew up on Beacon Hill. You bet I've got survival skills!*

Energized, I turned the key in the ignition with the assurance of a woman who knows how to take care of herself. Instead of wandering, directionless, I set a course to a hotel, the Regent Beverly Wilshire. The luxurious lobby instantly offered a familiar embrace, reminding me that I had been choosing hardship. Sumptuous surroundings were as much a part of my life experience as the poverty of my youth. In fact, I'd spent years, decades even, able to afford the "nice" things in life, yet this crisis had me sleeping in my car as if I were a little girl again. I plunked my credit card down for any room available.

In my hotel room, I slipped on the cushiony terrycloth robe, intending to head to the pool. Still somewhat shaken from the experience on the beach, I decided to look for a Gideon's Bible first. I found one in the desk drawer and flipped it open to Jeremiah. The appropriateness of the first words I read astonished me.

> But I will rescue you on that day, declares the LORD; you will not be handed over to those you fear. (Jer. 39:17)

That these words would be the first I'd see after physically running to escape what seemed to be dangerous guys on the beach made me think God was paying attention. And was once again directing words specifically to me. It made me feel sacred, a sensation so unusual it seemed everything around me sparkled with heightened beauty.

When I emerged onto the rooftop deck, I saw the city lights reflected in the pool. Orange silk draped the poolside cabanas, fluttering slightly in the warm air. Taking a step into the pool, I felt welcomed by the water. It was fully dark now, more than an hour since I'd awakened on the beach. Floating on my back, catching the few stars visible through the LA haze, I was reminded of the delight we kids felt when stargazing behind our grandparents' house in Idaho. We were safe, whenever we were there. And I was safe right here, under the stars at age fifty-two.

*God? Thank you.*

# Chapter 14

"Teddy's here!"

We run to the door like it's a holiday.

"Hey kids, want to go swimming?" she asks.

"Yay!"

We race upstairs to search for swimsuits. We stick our arms under beds and reach blindly up onto high closet shelves. We look in the kitchen, under the table. We dash to the basement, in case there's a swimming suit down there.

Carla finds a suit that's too tiny but she squeezes into it anyway, and won't give it up to Lotta or Baby, who might actually fit it. Annie puts on Mom's swimsuit, though the cups on the bra part fold in on themselves. All I can locate is a red skirt with suspenders, so I declare it a swimsuit. Eventually, we all have something to wear.

"Hooray, hooray for swimming," we chant, tumbling out the front door and climbing into Teddy's little blue car. With the youngest on the laps of the older ones and the windows rolled down, we take off to the lake, laughing, chattering, singing over each other.

Aunt Teddy doesn't tell us to be quiet, even when we ask questions like, "Are you an old maid?"

At Lake Washington, she spreads a blanket on the grass and watches us fly across the green to the shore where we plunge in, shrieking at the shock of cold water on a hot summer day. It is an invigorating relief that we didn't even know we needed.

## Bind up the Wounds

Relief was subtle. Though it seemed a kind of death had swept through and consumed everything I'd known to be true just months earlier, something was coming to life within me.

It didn't happen in a single moment, but over time I was choosing less and less to live at the mercy of someone else's actions. I began making plans, albeit short-term ones. Rather than driving aimlessly on weekends, I created getaways: hiking in Scottsdale, swimming at La Jolla cove, shopping in Santa Barbara, or dropping in to a spa. The first thing I did, in every resort or hotel, was find the Gideon's Bible.

That wasn't so easy during my week in Japan. I had visited several sites, including the cherry blossoms of Kyoto. On my last night, I was in an American hotel, a Sheraton, and thought surely they would have a Gideon's, but there was none in the room. Everyone at the front desk spoke flawless English, so I decided to call down and ask for one.

"Yes, ma'am," the polite man answered when I asked for a Bible. "We will send one to your room."

Several minutes later there was a knock on the door. The impeccably dressed steward held the book in both hands extended toward me and gave a slight bow.

I took the book, thanked him, and closed the door.

It was a room service menu.

Oh, well.

Once back in the states, I made my way through the entire book of Isaiah, then continued to another book, Psalms, which was full of comforting passages like, "He healeth the broken in heart, and bindeth up their wounds" (Ps. 147:3 KJV). There were also verses that fired me up, those in which God's wrath is called down upon enemies, like Psalm 34:16, "The face of the LORD is against those who do evil, to cut off the memory of them from the earth."

Admittedly, I indulged freely in the sentiment.

Every few days I returned to the house to spend a night or two, repack my suitcase, and get my mail.

"I just want to say how much I admire how you are walking through this horrible situation, which was not of your making. You have shown dignity, courage, and grace in this terrible situation that was thrust upon you. Love, Jeanie."

*Shall I display this?* I held the card from Jeanie in my hand, wondering if I should set it on the dining room shelf where we had routinely displayed Christmas, birthday, or anniversary cards. What does one do with a divorce card?

*Why not?*

Friends from Seattle sent one that read: "We're there for you. On that, you *can* depend."

From Minnesota came: "Love is not the falling, it's the *staying*."

Eventually, there were dozens of cards, lining three shelves in the dining room, each turned to face his seat at the head of the table. OK, maybe displaying the cards was small of me, but I was sick of the status quo. *Move out, already. Disappear.*


## Gone

People vanish. Numb, I learn not to get too close, love too much, or hold too tightly, but don't even know I'm learning these lessons because they're beyond what a young heart and mind can identify or express. Instead, the prospect that people might disappear is an unspoken and constant fear. My parents do it so often that it's actually more unsettling when they stick around. Aunt Teddy has left, gone far away to Guatemala. Now, one of us kids is about to depart too.

I am in the kitchen when Lilly shrieks, "Not that one!"

I drop the fork with a clatter onto the kitchen counter. Its prongs point at me.

"Annie used that one. Get another one."

We can't touch Annie's silverware, or any glass she uses, or any plate. I keep forgetting. And Carla keeps forgetting, and Lotta keeps forgetting, and Baby is too tiny to know. John and Lilly scold us.

"We told you not to use anything she touches."

"But, there aren't any more clean forks," I say.

"Then use a spoon. Make sure it's not one that Annie used."

But I don't know which spoon Annie used.

After weeks of us getting mixed up, Mom takes fingernail polish and paints a "J" on a fork, spoon, knife, plate, cup, and glass that are reserved for Jo Ann.

It's so we won't die. During the school's TB test, Annie's arm turned red. Now we're all scared of catching it and dying.

"She was only twenty-two," Mom says somberly as she takes us on a drive to see the old Indian Hospital where her own sister, Lilly, died of TB. We park, and everyone peers out the car window at the brick building on the hill. I can't help thinking how odd it is that I have a sister named Lilly and Mom had a sister named Lilly.

"I wonder if all families have sisters named Lilly," I say.

Annie jabs me in the ribs with her elbow.

"Lilly was named after Mom's dead sister, you idiot," she hisses.

Mom shows us a picture of the first Lilly. She looks like Mom but a tiny bit prettier, I think, and immediately feel guilty for the thought. We pass around the black and white photo of the Lilly who died while stealing glances at our own Lilly. One by one we cautiously peek at Annie, who incredibly, unbelievably, might have TB. It's beyond my imagining that she could get sick since she's always been the toughest, fastest tomboy. *Hey, "TB" could stand for tomboy,* I realize and almost point out the funniness of that but, afraid to say something dumb again, I keep quiet. When Mom begins to cry, we all drop our gazes, bringing our own arms into view. Unconsciously, we start checking them to make sure they're not getting a red bump like Annie's did.

On our next "Wake up, we're going to Idaho" trip, we leave Annie there.

It's so we won't get TB.

Annie runs up the narrow staircase into the attic space of our grandparents' house, which has been fixed up as a bedroom with white plastered walls and screened windows that look down on locust trees and green fields. She gets the bedroom all to herself. No more crowded mattress on the floor; hers is a real bed with springs and a white metal headboard. There's a painted white dresser against the wall, and a matching small white vanity with a mirror and a stool in front of it, just like in the movies. Annie gets rivers to swim in, and apple pies baked by Grandma. She gets a grandfather who shows her how to chop wood and fire a BB gun.

Driving away with Mom sniffling over her dead sister and her left-behind daughter, I get up on my knees and twist around to peer out the back window of the car at our grandparents' pale pink house diminishing in the distance, and I wish it were my arm that had turned red.

## The Shakes

Her arms transfix us. We watch in fascination as Mrs. Berg spills her drink time and again, her hands and arms seemingly uncontrollable. She's at the table with Mom, where they've been drinking some kind of booze that requires pouring into glasses; however, Mrs. Berg's hands shake so badly the liquid splashes out of the glass before she can get it to her lips.

We lean forward in anticipation. She's going to try another refill. Both arms fly about, as one hand grasps the bottle and the other seeks the cap. Her hands jerk every which way, meeting just long enough to unscrew the top.

As the pouring begins, her poached face is fierce in slippery concentration. Booze splatters onto the tabletop as she overfills the glass. Hands flying wide, she tries to prevent the spill, but the escaping liquid can't be recaptured. It glistens on the table in a growing puddle. As I watch it, I'm reminded of Teddy's words: "my cup runneth over."

Mrs. Berg grasps the full glass one more time, her hand shaking back and forth, sloshing more over the edge as she lifts it to her lips. We can't take our eyes off her. Even as little kids, we know it's the alcohol that gives Mrs. Berg the outrageous shakes. Our eyes shift to Mom, who seems unaware of her drinking partner's problem. We study Mom's hands, our eyes alert for any indication of a tremble. Seeing they're steady, we exhale, and lean into each other. Neither woman notices the four young girls watching them drink their poison.

# Chapter 15

Like Jo Ann's TB test, sometimes something happens that suddenly shifts things. In my divorce year, the shift was sharp. It happened when someone finally broke the news to me, while holding my hand across a small table in a busy café.

"I couldn't live with myself, knowing that I knew something and didn't tell you. He . . . uh . . . he has not been faithful."

The speaker's hand began to tremble in mine. It took one beat to notice the nervousness, another to note the calm in my own hand, and a third to decipher the meaning of the words. Once unleashed, the information flowed like something spilled across the tabletop, drenching me. Yet rather than feeling stained, I felt washed and somehow buoyant.

I walked away light on my feet, practically floating, and aware the sensation was oddly inappropriate.

*Infidelity. And I'm buoyed?*

I felt a kooky freedom—unfettered, as if some giant pair of scissors had cut the last threads that connected me to . . . what? My own denial. All the signs were there. But I had needed to really *hear* it before the truth I knew became the truth I believed.

As I drifted to my car, my lilting step made me feel like a fancy dancer at an Indian powwow, spinning and kicking in gravity-defying moccasins. Once inside the vehicle, my inner dance was too powerful to remain cramped in a car. I had to get out and walk around some more. Pacing the parking lot, the drumbeat in my head alternated, from a beat of "How dare you" to one that sang, "Thank God, I'm free."

*Free. Yes, free. It's time to take action.*

Punching the numbers into my cell phone, I noticed that my hands had belatedly begun to tremble. I thought that was a good thing.

"Good afternoon," said the receptionist at my lawyer's office.

"Please get Tina on the phone," I said, loudly. "And tell her it's Hattie calling. Tell her I want to file for divorce, right now. Today."

"Please hold."

*I don't want to hold. I've been holding way too long.*

## Laugh As They Skip

A letter arrives from Teddy. Aching for her, I carry it around and bring the envelope to school to show my teacher the stamp from Guatemala. I brag that I have an aunt who is a missionary in a faraway place.

At recess, three girls from my class giggle as they skip away, looking back at me. Thinking it's a game, I run after them, my sockless too-big shoes thudding against the concrete of the school ground. My classmates dip into some greenery next to the chain-link fence behind the portables. Excited at the hide-and-seek of it, I duck down and follow them into the brush.

"Hey," I say, uncovering them crouched behind a branch.

"Get out of here," Gail shrieks.

"Yeah, we're having a club meeting," Yvonne says.

"What's the club?" I ask.

Jamie rolls her eyes and deadpans, "It's the I Hate Hattie Club."

I don't feel myself walk away. I don't feel much of anything until I'm at home later with my sisters and become thoughtlessly mean. I tell Carla to shut up and push Lotta off a chair because I want to sit there. Though I'm the Boss and am supposed to watch the Kids, I get up and walk out the front door, leaving them alone.

For four blocks I keep up a steady pace until I get to the neat brick house where Yvonne lives. I knock, not considering what I might do if her mom answers. At the sound of footsteps coming to the door, my heart rises in my chest. The door opens to Yvonne's surprised face and my arm flies up to smack her. It's a slap. But my next strike is a punch. She pushes the door to lock it against me, but I'd landed the blows I'd meant to deliver. I feel better as I stroll home.

The next morning, I catch Gail in the grocery store a block from school. She's in the rear, near the coolers of milk, pop, and beer.

"Hi, Gail," I say, pushing her backward toward the door of the cooler.

Before she can call for help, I shove her inside where no one can see us. It is dim and cold behind the racks of bottles, when I let my fists fly. She's crying as I walk out of the cooler, closing the heavy metal door behind me.

In class, I stare at Jamie's back when she raises her hand to answer Teacher's questions. I am waiting for the bell to signal recess.

"It's a fight!" the boys yell, quickly circling us.

It really isn't a fight. It's just me, whacking Jamie right and left.

"Get her, Hattie, get her," the boys shout, until it's broken up by two teachers.

*I've put an end to the I Hate Hattie Club*, I think, as I'm pulled off Jamie.

## Enough

I filed for divorce.

Or rather, my lawyer did it for me. I made the phone call, and two days later the court made it official: wife seeks divorce from husband. Wife has had enough. It was perhaps a week later when I got the call from the attorney's office.

"He's been served."

I swelled at the words.

# Chapter 16

The meaning of "Wake up, we're going to Idaho" is different now. It means we're off to visit Annie, who is still in TB quarantine at our grandparents' house. We spring from bed, happy for the chance to see our sister. If we're visiting in winter, we'll slide down the snowy field on Annie's sled, dodging shrubs and trees. If it happens to be a summer visit, we'll float and bob on the river, fighting for a chance to grab on to Annie's inner tube. Regardless of season, it's always good news to hear we're heading to Idaho.

There, we eat three bountiful meals in a single day: eggs and bacon at breakfast; meat and potatoes, hot fry bread with home-made berry jam, and milk to drink at lunch. And all of that comes back again at supper, plus Grandma's pie for dessert. Grandpa chuckles, watching us wolf down the food.

He calls Annie "Kut Kut," an Indian word that means *small* in an endearing sense, like she's a small version of Mom, or maybe a small version of him. When he chops wood with an axe, he lets her try it with a hatchet. When he puts Brylcreem on his hair, she copies him, slicking back her bangs with the goop.

On this visit, we get nicknames too. He calls Lotta "Shorty," and names me "Howcome." I stop myself from asking how come

I have to have a name like that. I want something cute or clever or affectionate and all I get is a name that basically means, "Why?"

We don't stay long, since this trip was a midnight impulse and we didn't pack clothes. And it's not a school holiday, or even a weekend. As we get ready to go, Grandma hands Mom some USDA commodity surplus food. It's not oatmeal this time, but a bag of powdered eggs, a box of powdered milk, a can of shortening, and a large sack of flour. Seeing the supplies, I imagine Lilly making green eggs and blue milk, but those mental images are interrupted because we're being herded to the car. Piling in, we yell our farewells.

"Bye, Annie!"

"Scoot over."

"Stop pushing."

"I want the window."

"Shut up. That's my seat."

## Heritage

Buckling my seat belt, I looked down at my hands and noticed again the strange nicks that had appeared on my knuckles overnight. I didn't remember hitting my hand on anything, but there were two or three small scabs, as if I'd punched someone. Mom would probably say it was Indian medicine, like I'd put a hex on someone and pummeled them from miles away.

The plane lifted off from LAX and swung out over the ocean before turning north toward Seattle. My youngest sister, Claudia, had won election to the legislature and was to be sworn in: the first Native American woman ever elected to the Washington State Senate. I knew that before the weekend was out I'd hear Indian drumming. I'd feel the power of Coyote, the magical trickster revered by my tribe for his ability to resurrect himself time and again; Coyote, who had fought the monster and lived.

According to Nez Perce legend, before there were human beings the animals walked and talked freely with one another. One day a new and different animal appeared, one with a voracious appetite. The new animal stopped first at Raccoon's house.

"I'm hungry," it said.

"Well, sit right down," answered Raccoon. "I'll cook you a meal."

After the new creature ate all that Raccoon could cook, it was still hungry.

"But, you've eaten all I have," said Raccoon. "There's no more food."

"Then I will eat your children," snarled the beast, springing at the kids.

Raccoon fled in terror and grief, warning the other animals about the new creature they soon called the Monster. Nothing could stop it. It ate and ate, growing larger all the while.

The animals called an emergency council.

"We have to stop it before it devours us all," cried Deer.

"How can we stop it?" asked Bear. "Its mouth is so big now, it can swallow me whole."

"Only Coyote has the power to stop it," suggested Fox.

The animals fretted over calling Coyote. It was true he had magical powers, but his schemes often backfired. Still, something had to be done, and so they took the chance and summoned Coyote.

*Hmm*, Coyote thought, sitting in the sun on a hillside above the river. *So, they want me to kill a monster.* Like any animal, he had insecurities, especially about taking on a monster. But he was Coyote. He had already brought fire to the others. He had danced with the Star sisters in the sky. He had even traveled to the land of the dead once, though that hadn't turned out so well.

Just as he was ruminating on whether he was brave or cowardly when it came to monsters, there it was, floating down the river. The

Monster had grown so large that its mouth stretched almost from bank to bank as it swallowed up all of the Salmon.

Without taking time to think, Coyote leaped for the water, using his magic to turn himself into a stick, which floated on the surface and was gulped up immediately by the beast. Once in the Monster's stomach, Coyote used his magic to turn himself back into himself.

"Hey, Coyote," shouted the animals, still alive in there. "Save us!"

Coyote pulled his knife from the sheath at his belt and began hacking away at the Monster's insides. In time, the Monster felt these blows and tried to crawl out of the river. It came to rest on the shore, dying, as Coyote sliced away, eventually making a hole large enough for the animals to escape the Monster's body.

"Yay, yay for Coyote." They began to dance and sing.

Raven, flying low overhead, sounded a warning.

"What if the Monster comes back to life?" he asked.

"Well, I'll cut it into tiny pieces," answered Coyote, annoyed at Raven for dampening the scene.

"What if the pieces grow back together?" asked Raven on another flyby.

*Oh, darn Raven*, thought Coyote.

"Well, I'll cut it into tiny pieces, and then throw the pieces far from one another, so it can't grow back together," yelled Coyote. And with that, he began to fling pieces of the Monster's flesh.

And a strange thing happened. Every time the Monster's flesh came into contact with the earth, from that spot came Human Beings. And in that way, the tribes were placed upon the earth. Coyote dispersed the Monster's body until all that remained was the heart. And this he raised over his head and dashed to the ground, right there along the Clearwater River, and from that very spot came the Nez Perce Indians, who speak from the heart.

Grandpa taught us that story. I remember wondering how come no one got digested. When my grandson Phoenix first heard the tale, he said, "Hey, Grammie, that means we're all part Monster, doesn't it?"

And I recalled that my brother, John, used the Coyote and Monster story in the play he wrote before he died. I looked out the airplane window at the snow-covered mountains below. We were over Oregon now, and that meant beyond those forested mountains in the distance was Idaho and the Nez Perce reservation, with the Clearwater River and the mound next to it, which we were always told was the Monster's heart.

Admiring the jagged peaks and twisting valleys, I felt a growing sense of myself, as if I were a part of the rugged country below. When the Nez Perce went to war in 1877, they climbed over the mountains, crossed rushing rivers, and fought running battles through the wilderness until, outgunned, they were forced to surrender to the US Cavalry. But not all of them. White Bird's band never gave up. The spirited fighters and their families slipped into Canada for safety, and then slowly, slyly, some of them snuck back into America to blend in with the Indians on the reservation.

In his surrender, Chief Joseph is recorded saying, "From where the sun now stands, I shall fight no more forever." White Bird never made a surrender speech, because they never got him. With my nose pressed against the airplane window, I silently mouthed the words, "From where the sun now stands, I am ready to fight."

The next day I stood with my sisters in the gallery of the Washington State Senate. When newly elected Senator Claudia Kauffman was called forward, we erupted into cheers and war whoops for Baby.

"I see you brought some friends along," said the chief justice of the State Supreme Court, glancing up at us.

Carla grabbed my hand as Claudia took her oath of office. Lilly wiped a tear. Jo Ann whispered, "What do you think Mom and Dad would say if they could see this?"

No one had to speak of how our deprivation and spunky survival stood in such contrast to this moment—but I'm sure a different image flashed in each of our minds, a memory, an experience, a word that grounded each of us to a point in the past and made the present emerge in stark relief as we watched the baby of the family achieve something our parents would never have imagined. I wondered how we would celebrate if they were still with us.


## Celebration

I've waited for this celebration for weeks. It's my birthday and the best part is Mom and Dad are home. Sober. We sit at the table at dinner, eating mush, talking and laughing like a family is supposed to. I kick my legs under my chair, giddy that everyone's here and that my birthday has brought Mom and Dad home. After a bit, Mom stands up and goes back into the kitchen. I wiggle and try to contain my grin, certain she's getting a birthday cake ready for me.

A few seconds later, the door to the kitchen swings open to reveal her face illuminated by candlelight. The little flames reflect in her dark eyes.

"Happy birthday to you," they sing, lifting me into the rapture of a little girl turning five. Beaming, I stretch up to get a good look at my cake.

What? The candles are sticking out of . . . another bowl of . . . mush.

"Happy birthday, dear Hattie. Happy birthday to you."

"How come?"

Before I can finish my question everyone bursts out laughing.

"Blow out your candles," they say. "Make a wish!"

Should I wish for a cake?

I look up at my family—confused because their faces don't reflect what I feel. No one seems disappointed or surprised by the birthday mush. They are happier than I remember seeing any of them in a very long time. Dad has his arm around Mom and they're both smiling at me.

"Make a wish," Mom urges.

I close my eyes and wish for more dinners like this one. I blow out the secondhand stubs of candles sinking into mush.

I am happy.

## Feast

Steaks, salmon, and rich desserts filled the table at our celebration for the new state senator. Her husband raised his glass and said, "It is an honor to be Claudia's husband, an honor to be married into this great family."

Immediately, Carla's husband echoed the sentiment, adding that we were a strong and resilient bunch, and that it was his privilege to be associated with our family.

*Had mine ever said anything like that?*

I began to feel a detachment from the room. The talk around the table continued but I pulled back, remembering a day fifteen years earlier. My husband and I had been visiting the sisters on the reservation. A bunch of us were gathered in Carlotta's house, and the leaky kitchen sink had gotten on my husband's nerves, so he'd taken it upon himself to fix it.

As we sisters sat in the kitchen laughing and telling stories, he was on the floor, his head obscured under the sink, his long, thin legs stretching into the room. Carlotta and the rest of us gabbed on. We were all there except for the sister who had recently married a man that none of us approved of, a tall Sioux with a mean streak.

"Is she still in Seattle?" Lilly asked.

"No." Carlotta shook her head. "She and What's-His-Name are on their way to South Dakota."

Clang . . . came the sound from under the sink.

"I can't stand that guy," said another sister.

Bang . . . went wrench against pipe.

Later, in our motel room, my husband complained bitterly about what he'd overheard.

"What's-His-Name?" he demanded. "Is that what your sisters call me, too? Is that what every man who marries into this family is called? What's-His-Name?"

"No," I tried to explain. "It's just that nobody likes this guy."

The next day, when I was alone with my sisters, I told them about his hurt feelings and asked them to be especially nice to him. They met this with surprise and regret at our loose talk, but within minutes, one of them giggled.

"Got to get going. Time to cook dinner for What's-His-Name."

One joke was followed by the next, and before we knew it, we were five women keeled over in laughter.

"What are you and What's-His-Name doing for Christmas?"

"Did you hear about Carla and What's-His-Name?"

It became one of our running gags. Of course, anytime the sisters were together, there were belly laughs. We didn't need much to get us going.

A sudden burst of laughter brought me back to our group in the restaurant. A plate of food sat uneaten in front of me. I shook off the memories and admired the happy faces all around: my sisters and their loving husbands.

*This is family. Thank you, God.*

"Remember the time we survived on raw spaghetti?" Claudia mimed holding a dry noodle to her mouth. "Crunch, crunch." Despite the story of seven of us dividing up uncooked spaghetti noodles, Claudia, the new state senator once known as Baby, remembers our home life as "a working-class family with parents committed to their children and to their community."

The first time I heard her say this, I thought, *Are you kidding?* I returned to my desperate moment of scraping jam with my fingertip and holding it to her mouth. But, of course, her impression of our upbringing would be unlike mine. By the time Baby was in

elementary or middle school, our parents had settled down. Dad
was the provider. Mom stayed home with the Kids. We were long
out of the Projects and into our second house. John would have
been in college by then, acting in or directing plays. Lilly would
have been travelling with an American Indian dance group, win-
ning first place at powwows and even riding on a float as a princess
during Seattle's annual Sea-Fair parade. It was a different life. Since
Claudia had been an infant and toddler when our family hit bottom as our parents' marriage erupted in the Projects, she probably
didn't have memories of the havoc that ensued. She would recall
instead the well-read Dad who discussed local politics and rarely
missed a day of work, and the Mom who joined an American
Indian women's service group and took a class at the community
park on flower arranging.

Yet these same parents had failed in the worst way during my
most formative years. No wonder I grew up to become a reporter,
one who seeks information and is driven to find answers that might
help make sense of situations that make no sense at all. Reporters
ask who-what-where-why-how. From the time I could talk, those
were my questions: Who? (is in charge of us), What? (is going on),
Where? (are they), When? (will they come home), Why? (did they
leave), How? (are we going to make it). In a little girl's vocabulary,
all of that was condensed into the question, "How come?"

But that was me. This night was about Claudia, and it did,
indeed, culminate in Indian drumming. Tribes from throughout
the state celebrated "Baby's" victory. Her picture would grace the
front page of the paper in the morning. Later, snug in a suite at
the Alexis Hotel, amid the upscale shops and restaurants of First
Avenue, I looked down at the street below and remembered when
it had been called skid row, the site of escapades; Mom getting
beat up by three guys who didn't like the look of her, Dad falling
off the pier into frigid Puget Sound.

*But no, Hattie, also remember the good things.*

128

Suddenly, I recalled Mom's love of nice clothes. "Gotta look sharp," she'd say. It wasn't just the attire. It was what it represented: that we had made it, that we belonged, that we were as good as anyone else. I remembered a time from my teenage years, when she'd asked me to drive her downtown because she needed to make a deposit in the bank. The small outlying branches wouldn't do. She wanted to walk into Seattle's first skyscraper, a narrow black rectangle so out of place among the low-lying buildings that people joked, "It looks like the box the Space Needle came in." But to Mom, the new high-rise was symbolic of wealth, stature, and success. The fact that she had an account with the bank that built it meant somehow that the new high-rise was partially hers. Mom had dressed up for the occasion, in a suit and heels, her hair curled just so. I recalled watching her step across the courtyard to enter the building, her purse hooked on her arm, holding the check that was her entry ticket, and I knew in that moment, *My mom is happy; right now, she is happy.*

Feeling tears, I turned away from the hotel window view of the former skid row, now gentrified and redeemed. I was beginning to sense that redemption might always be there, in every situation, if you just stretch out further and reach a little higher.

# Chapter 17

There were lots of families as hungry as we were. In the 1950s and '60s, American Indians ventured off the reservation, drawn to the possibility of work in the cities or forced to make their way because of government policy at the time to terminate reservations. *Assimilation* was the watchword of the day, and it could be argued that the dislocation provided opportunities for better education and jobs. But the downside was deep. Families, no matter how poor, had a natural safety net on reservations in the form of extended relations, the network of cousins and grandmas and uncles who could offer food or a place to sleep. A traditionalist might add "Cousin Deer" or "Brother Salmon" to that list of relatives, because they represented sustenance from hunting and fishing.

But the midcentury Indian families who moved to the city found themselves alone, far from the support of relatives and with no way to forage food from the land. This was before Lyndon Johnson's Great Society, welfare, AFDC, and food stamps. Though USDA surplus commodity food was available on the reservation, there was no food assistance for Native American families in the city. Hungry homes remained hungry, and often, isolated.

## Shiny Shoes

"They're here. They're here!"

We dash out the front door and down the steps to the sidewalk to meet Grandpa's pickup truck. Grandma smiles through the passenger window and Annie waves from her seat between them. They've come from Idaho to visit us.

As Grandma offers Mom a box of commodity food, Annie hops out of the truck, revealing a pair of shiny black shoes on her feet. They're the kind Candy wore in the Projects, patent leather with a little strap across the top.

Everyone greets one another with laughter and hellos, but I'm speechless over the shoes. We used to try to beat up Candy because of shoes like that.

Inside, the house has been swept clean and Mom and Dad are on their best behavior. School is out for Easter vacation and Annie's home to visit because she's not dying of TB. She never even got sick from it. (In adulthood, she'll tell us the red bump on her arm was probably a mosquito bite, not a positive TB test result as we all thought it was.)

Grandma and Grandpa stay overnight, just long enough to rest before driving back to Idaho.

"You got taller," I say to Annie. *And tougher*, I think to myself.

She displaces me as the Boss of the little ones. Lotta and Carla switch allegiance immediately, but Baby still runs to me. Baby and I get slaughtered in a shoe war by Annie, Carla, and Lotta.

I resent being pushed aside from my leadership post over the little ones, and I am jealous of Annie's strength and of the general excitement over her presence. Yet at the same time, I'm just as excited as everyone else. I love her tremendously and wish I could be exactly like her. I want to be tough, and clever, and have shiny shoes. Inevitably, we fight. Inevitably, she wins. She can out-punch and out-wrestle me, but I leave scratch marks on the skin of her forearms, my only weapons being my fingernails and my refusal to give up.

131

John and Lilly are still home and part of the family, but because they're teenagers, it's almost like they're not in our world anymore. It's me and the Kids, and now, Annie.

One afternoon, she comes in with a fistful of daffodil and tulip sprouts in her hand, the bulbs that Aunt Teddy and I had planted last year, dangling from the thin green shoots.

"Look Hattie, your onions are ripe."

"Those aren't onions," I say, thinking she's so silly. "They're flowers."

I shake my head, marveling that there could be something in the world that Annie doesn't know. As I begin explaining what bulbs are and how you're supposed to plant them in the fall for flowers to come up in the spring, she laughs and says, "Oops, sorry. I thought they were onions."

Later, when Mom lines us up at the sink to wash our hair with Naphtha laundry soap, she notices that Annie doesn't have any lice or nits.

"Must be the Brylcreem," Mom mutters. "I guess it kills the eggs."

Annie is still using Grandpa's hair slicker. She is the only one who puts goop on her hair like he does. After the shampoo, Annie squirts Brylcreem from her tube and with both hands smooths it over her still-wet head of hair, while the rest of us watch.

"Thou anointest my head with oil," I recall Teddy telling me.

"What does that mean?" I asked.

"It's a blessing," Teddy said. "It's a way people blessed one another, with oil."

"Blessing?"

"Yes. You've heard that word before. When people say 'God bless you,' they're saying may God protect you, keep you, and favor you."

I watch my special sister, the one who gets TB and doesn't die, the one who can shove me around while grinning, the one who doesn't get lice, and has her own bedroom and shoes like Candy's, and I decide that Brylcreem must be the way she anoints herself. Certainly, she is blessed.

## God Was Involved

The warm oil felt good on my scalp.

"You don't mind if your hair gets greasy?"

"Not at all," I mumbled to the masseuse, my face pressed into the tiny crevice of the massage table. I was in Hawaii, giving myself a break from the LA routine of sneaking in and out of the house. The divorce was inching forward as winter turned into spring.

I splashed in the brilliant blue water of Poi Pu beach early one morning, not noticing at first that a young man was watching me.

"Hi," he called. "Do this every day?"

"On vacation," I answered, feeling loosened by the salt water. "I might even buy a surf lesson today."

"I could teach you for free. In five minutes I could have you surfing."

"Seriously?"

"Easy. I could teach you this very minute," he guaranteed.

His skin was tanned a deep bronze. He was about thirty years old, buff, with green eyes and sun-bleached, sandy hair; clearly, no mainland tourist.

"Really?" I asked.

"Let's do it," he urged.

Minutes later, I was lying on his surfboard, my face pointed toward the shoreline. He stood behind me, in water up to his chest, holding the tail of the board with both hands. A bit embarrassed that my rear end was facing him, I glanced back, but he wasn't looking at me. His face was turned to the wave rolling toward us.

"Paddle now. Paddle fast."

He pushed me forward with the wave.

"Stand up, stand up," he called. Adrenaline took over. First one knee came forward, then the other. I stood and balanced on the board as it skimmed over the blue.

*I'm surfing!*

The exhilaration lasted all of five seconds before I fell off the board. But feeling gleefully successful, I paddled back out.

"I knew you could do it," he said before pushing me into the next wave. After four or five runs, I asked him if he wanted a turn. He shook his head.

"What I really need is a job." He turned his face toward the horizon that had held the sunrise, which was no longer a shocking orange but had shifted into a pink blue.

"A job?" I asked, somewhat distracted by the little droplets of water sparkling on his chest.

"I just got out of jail." He turned his green eyes back to meet mine.

"Oh."

*I'm surfing with someone who just got out of jail.*

I quickly mumbled something about needing to get back to my friends, trying to emphasize the *friends* part, as if I were not traveling alone. His eyes called my bluff.

"One more," he pressed. "Turn around, here comes a wave."

I floated along the speeding water, feeling giddy from both the swift movement and my recklessness in the waves with someone who could be dangerous.

*If I were still "happily married" . . . would I be surfing with a guy who just got out of jail? No. Then again, would I be surfing at all?*

That perspective freed me from fear, and as I glided toward shore, I felt that I was free to live by different rules—and that, maybe, God was involved. I still had no idea what all the God-stuff meant, but I felt a peaceful openness to seeing it through.

Unleashing the board from my ankle, I gave a smile of gratitude to the young, gorgeous ex-prisoner.

"You know what?" I asked spontaneously. "They charge forty or fifty dollars an hour for surf lessons. Could I pay you for teaching me?"

"No." He shrugged.

"Where have you been staying since you got out of jail?"

"On the beach," he admitted. "There are showers." He lifted his chin to point to the bathhouse.

Earlier, I'd admired his six-pack waist, not thinking, until now, that it might be the result of hunger.

"Take twenty dollars," I said with finality. We'd broken through embarrassment. "You helped me today."

"Hey, you're helping me." He smiled. "Now I can get some breakfast."

Knowing that I was putting food in someone's belly gave me a lift, a joy that felt fresh and new. Leaving the beach, I wondered what puts one person in another's path, and immediately had to laugh at myself. "God does, of course."

After the Psalms, I had begun reading the New Testament. Perhaps the Bible reading was beginning to pervade my thinking, I considered, as I pulled out of the beach parking lot. The old me would have freaked out and run away upon learning the guy had been in jail, and the new me hadn't even asked why he was arrested. Shaking my head at myself, I noticed, to my right, a ramshackle building with a hand-painted sign: "Stuff for Sale." Recalling that I hadn't brought a Bible on this Hawaii trip, I decided to stop to see if there might be one among the stuff. A roughened blonde woman with sun-damaged skin gave me a wry smile when I asked. She disappeared into the back and returned with an old, white, leather-bound version.

"How much?"

"Oh, I don't charge for the Good Book," she croaked in the voice of a longtime smoker. Both her crusty appearance and voice might normally have repelled me, but my eyes were opened by her generosity and the nature of her gift, so I smiled and thanked her.

"God bless you, sister," she wheezed after me.

## That Fruit I Keep

When I'm in the fifth grade, we move to our next house, one so creepy looking that when a classmate spots us carrying boxes up the concrete steps, he calls out, "Hey, Hattie, you guys moving into the haunted house?" Its faded wooden shingles hang askew. A broken window upstairs is patched, which makes the house look like it's winking at the world. Next door is an empty, overgrown lot.

Mom isn't with us when we move because she's in the hospital. Her sickness is called Lupus. John looks it up in a dictionary and tells us *lupus* means "wolf," which only makes the whole thing seem more scary. We're in a haunted house and our mom has a wolf disease.

In the first day or two after the move, I wander outside, stepping over ivy and sticker bushes, drawn to a tree that's barely alive. It doesn't have any leaves on it, but looking up, I notice something golden: a peach. I begin to climb, my knees shinnying up the dark, rough bark. The last branch thick enough to hold me is still well below the peach. I must stretch, leaning out into space, one foot balanced on the limb, my hand grasping up into the sky for the fruit.

Got it.

Juice slips down my chin as I savor the taste—sweet, tart, and wild. Too soon it is gone. Clinging to the gnarled branch, I marvel at my luck in finding a peach, the only peach, and the double thrill of not having to share it with everyone. I drop the wrinkled pit to the ground, wishing it would grow a new tree.

As I lean back against the wood, a feeling begins to enfold me. It is a warmth, at first, no more than that. As I concentrate on the sensation, it grows until I'm certain the warmth comes from . . . from being loved. *I am being loved.* It seems to surround me. My child's mind grows still and I see the intricacy of the bark before my eyes. An ant crawls across its surface. As I follow this tiny bit of life, I am aware of something tremendously large all around me. It is invisible, vast, and absolutely good. And it *loves* me. Me!

*It must be God*, I think. Aunt Teddy would tell me it's God, but I can't even give much thought to Aunt Teddy because this great big love feeling leaves no room for thoughts. I know, with all that I'm capable of knowing, that it is God. And I am loved.

"Hattie, get in here and help," my sister calls from the porch, breaking the moment.

Slipping down from the tree, I scratch my knee and announce my discovery while bolting up the front porch steps.

"We have a peach tree!"

"Where?"

"Come look. It's that tree right there."

"The dead one?"

"Yep, it had a peach."

"Where?"

"I ate it."

"Liar."

"I'm not lying. I dropped the pit right there."

We tromp through the tall grass and ivy to the twisted tree, but I can't spot the pit in the green undergrowth. It has disappeared as if it never existed.

"That tree's dead as a doornail."

"No. I mean, yeah, it does look dead. But it had a peach, a juicy—"

"Stop making things up."

"Get in here and help put things away."

The tree never bears another peach. Eventually Dad chops it down.

I don't tell anyone about God's embrace. That fruit I keep to myself.

# Chapter 18

"Mexico? I'm going to Mexico?"

In my hand is a letter from Teddy and a plane ticket.

"Why do you get everything?" Lotta snarls.

I ignore my little sister, still stunned that Aunt Teddy is inviting me to visit her at her new mission. She's left Guatemala and is now in Mexico, and has sent a plane ticket for me.

"I'm going to Mexico," I affirm to myself and to everyone in the room.

"You get to go abroad before I do?" asks John, incredulously.

"Does Mexico count as abroad?" Lilly says, taking the letter from my hand to examine it.

"I wanna go," says Baby, leaning against my leg. "I wanna go with you."

"Don't worry, I'll come back." I hug her.

In days, I'm on a plane, all by myself. "Braniff," say the signs. I am flying Braniff Airlines to see my aunt, I want to tell the stewardess, but she probably knows it's Braniff Airlines and that we're going to Mexico. *But she doesn't know Aunt Teddy*, I think, hugging myself.

Landing at the Mexico City airport, excitement turns to confusion because the signs are all in Spanish, and in a rush I realize I can't read a thing. Everyone talks loudly and I have no idea what they're saying, or what I'm supposed to do, or where I'm supposed to go. Caught up in the current, I follow the crowd through the concourses and hallways until we spill out into a large room. Because the crowd isn't moving anymore, I don't have a sense of which direction to walk. Fear begins to grab me, but just then, through a glass wall, I catch the face of my aunt scanning the crowd. I run to the glass partition where we exchange waves and big smiles. She points me to the sign in the big room where people are lining up and motions for me to join them, mouthing the words, "I'll wait right here." Even though I know I have to go line up to get out to her, I don't want to pull myself away from the view of her through the glass. Walking away, I keep turning around to make sure she's still there. My aunt is there. She cares about me. She's waving at me, and waiting for me.

But I am not the seven-year-old who memorized the Twenty-Third Psalm. I am eleven and hardened. Once we're settled in her rooms at the mission, I talk back to her and question why she's an old maid who has become a missionary. Disagreeable, I call the little village boring and complain there's no good music on the radio. They don't even have the Beatles. I ignore the Bible she gives me. I feel like beating somebody up, but at the same time, I'm too embarrassed to tell her about the I Hate Hattie Club.

Snooping about her small apartment one afternoon, I come upon her diary. I know I shouldn't open it, but I do, expecting some juicy tale of forbidden romance. *Now we'll get to the real reason she left us in Seattle*, I think. Instead, the first sentence crushes me.

"I am praying for the right words to say to Hattie . . ."

*She is praying for me?*

I close her journal, awash with shame at my ingratitude and immature behavior.

My emotions are jumbled: guilt at peeking into her journal, amazement that anyone would pray for me, love for Teddy, rebellion against doing what I'm told, wonder at who or what she prays to.

139

Our time together begins to change. I listen to her and try to do the right thing each day, making my bed in the morning and cleaning up the dishes after dinner. When I ask if there's anything else I can do to help out, Teddy smiles and says I should give some attention to the little barefoot child who shows up at the missionary compound each day.

I'd seen the girl hanging around, but hadn't given her any consideration because she looked only about four years old, too young for me to pal around with. But to please Teddy, now I smile at her when she arrives each day. Taking the time to examine the girl, I see her clothes aren't really dresses or pants, but look to be pieces of woven cloth wrapped around her like a towel. When I push her on the swing, I notice her brown, skinny legs are scabby. She mumbles in Spanish, so I try to learn some words, but we mostly communicate by pointing.

In the evenings, Teddy and I sit quietly reading. She tells me to start with the book of Matthew.

"So, *that's* why they call it the Lord's Prayer," I exclaim one night, over my Bible. "I always thought that was just the name of it: the Lord's Prayer. You know, like the Pledge of Allegiance. I didn't know it actually *came* from Jesus."

Sometimes, I think I see tears in Teddy's eyes as she watches me read.

Occasionally, she takes me with her to visit villagers who live in such poverty that, in comparison, our rickety house in Seattle is a mansion. What one family calls home is a mere square on the ground. The outline of the square is made of cactus growing in the desert sand. Some canvas or other material hangs between the tall cactus plants to make a roof, or at least a partial shade.

"That's their *house?*" I ask, after we've said our goodbyes.

"That's where they live," Teddy answers.

Walking back to the mission, we come upon a man squatting beside the dirt path.

"Keep walking," Teddy whispers to my gasp.

"But, he's pooping outside, in front of anybody who comes along."

"Not everyone has bathrooms," Teddy explains. "No, don't look back. Just keep walking."

"But that's disgusting."

"People are poor, Hattie. People are poor all over the world. What does Jesus say about the poor?"

My mind races back over Matthew. Blessed are the . . . but could she mean that guy near the path was blessed? I lean into Teddy as we walk along.

"I know, I know," I say eventually, even though I don't understand it at all. If the poor are blessed, does that mean the Kauffman kids are blessed? But even when we didn't have water, we had the gas station water six blocks away, so maybe we weren't really poor. And even without lights, we had a roof overhead and didn't have to sleep under the sky, in a square shape on the ground with cactus as walls. So our mattress caught on fire from the heater one time. So what? At least we kids had a heater. Sometimes.

On my twelfth birthday, Aunt Teddy wakes me by opening the window to mariachi music. Outside, three guys are playing guitars and singing "Feliz Cumpleanos." Recognizing the birthday song, I jump from bed and stick my head out the window. They wave, grinning widely, and keep playing for me.

"For me?" I shriek to Teddy. She nods, looking even happier than I feel. That afternoon she takes me into the tiny town, where a lady curls and pins up my long hair, making me feel grown-up and pretty. We stop at a shack where another lady sells fabric.

"Let's sew you a dress," Teddy says.

When I can't decide between two fabrics, she buys a yard and a half of each. At home, in our cinderblock rooms of the missionary compound, she cuts the fabric, pins, and sews, and in a couple days I have two new dresses. It's the first time in my life that I have two new dresses, and it's not even the start of the school year.

I take turns wearing each one to the tiny church that's not really a church, but rather a room in the compound where the missionaries and the people who live nearby in the cactus homes come to sing once a week. The little barefoot girl brings her barefoot mom, who also wears the colorful woven cloth.

In the heat of Mexico, I relax into the rhythm of the days: the child to play with, Spanish lessons, Jesus lessons, meals with Teddy, joining her on her walks to visit the cactus people, reading together at night, and saying our prayers.

After a couple of months the mission ends and we begin driving north, touring as we go. The paper road map has a picture of a pyramid on it, and when I ask if we can see it, she plots a course that takes us to the sun pyramid near Mexico City. Together we climb to the top of it and hold hands, looking out on what used to be an Indian city.

One day, during our road trip north to America, I tell her I always wanted to ride a horse. She finds a horse ranch. With bravado, I announce that I don't want a horse to just walk, or trot. I only want a horse that gallops.

"How do I ask for a horse that runs?"

"Un caballo que corre."

The small dark man in the cowboy hat nods when I demand, "Un caballo que corre, un caballo que corre."

I'm barely into the saddle when the horse bolts, galloping in a determined line away from the ranch and into the desert. Its long neck stretches out with each stride, and its hooves thunder below. *Guppity, guppity, guppity.* I lose the reins first. Then the saddle vanishes beneath me and I'm airborne. With a thud, I land amid cactus so sharp its spines penetrate not only my jeans but the soles of my shoes.

The Mexican man and Teddy run to me, but I'm not hurt, except for the pricks of cactus. Brushing off the dust, and removing the needles, we little by little begin to chuckle. Lifting his skinny shoulders, the Mexican man explains, "Un caballo que corre."

Proudly exhausted, I limp to the car like a cowboy hero, and lean my head against Teddy as we drive away. I've ridden a galloping horse and I am alive. As if in celebration of my accomplishment, a radio station finally plays a Beatles song, the Spanish-speaking DJ pronouncing it, "Los Beet-Les." I turn up the volume, and sing aloud to the Beatles while Teddy smiles at the road ahead.

As we cross the border into America on a particularly hot day, I remark how good it would feel to jump into a cool pool. That night, Teddy finds a motel with a small swimming pool in its parking lot. Struck by her many acts of kindness, I steal looks at her, as if I am suddenly shy in the presence of someone new to me. *She seems too good to be a real person*, I think, watching her get the key at the front desk. But my awkwardness disappears as quickly as it began, and is forgotten with the first plunge into the cool water.

Driving across Texas, we discuss kindness. She says that Jesus wants us to be kind to others, that our greatest command is to love God and to love our neighbors. And that everyone is our neighbor, even people we don't like. At night, before climbing into our twin beds in one motel after another, we say prayers, asking God to take care of us and protect us. And we pray for Mom, Dad, John, Lilly, Annie, Carla, Lotta, and Baby. I go to sleep happy.

When we see a sign that says "Welcome to Oklahoma City," Teddy tells me our road trip is done. She has to stay there for missionary training, and because she has to be in school every day, I can't stay with her. And besides, it's time for me to go back to Seattle to get ready for the sixth grade. And my family must miss me.

At the airport, we hold each other tightly and cry. I delay boarding the plane, but finally, I have to walk away from her. Looking back over my shoulder, I wave and wave. It is the last time I see Aunt Teddy.

## The Most Valuable Thing

Decades later, I again found myself in the midst of great poverty and need in Mexico. It was a work assignment that made me think of Teddy the entire time. Thin-legged kids mobbed us when we got out of our rental car at the Mexico City garbage dump. After six years of reporting and anchoring in Seattle, I was hired by ABC's *Good Morning America* and this was one of my first international assignments. We'd come to do a story about the thirty thousand people who live around the dump, scavenging daily for their existence.

The second we opened the car door, the smell of the garbage oppressed us. Skeletal arms reached up, begging for food. Ruefully regretting that I hadn't considered buying food on the way to the shoot, I searched through my pockets for anything to hand out, finding only a small bag of airline peanuts, a pitiful offering in the face of such hunger.

The immense need surrounding our camera crew made it nearly impossible to focus on the work we were sent to do.

"How are we going to tell this story?" I moaned to the producer.

"I have an idea, Hattie," he said. "How about if we ask each person to show us the most valuable thing they own. And then we'll string together a series of the images in a montage. It'll be great."

I cringed at his suggestion, fearing that it might be demeaning to the people. How would they respond to us, in our caravan of rental cars and expensive camera gear, asking them to pull out their most valuable tin cup or sheet of corrugated metal to display? Even though he didn't mean it that way, it seemed to me that this plan would mock their poverty.

"It'll be great," he pressed. "You'll see."

We set up for our first interview. The woman facing us was thin and tired looking. She stood on bare ground in front of a hovel made of pieces of plastic, cardboard, and a torn, partial sheet of particleboard. Barefoot kids darted around her on the dirt, which glinted in the sun from flecks of metal or glass. Flies buzzed.

When we were finally ready, I asked her, through an interpreter, where she came from, why she had traveled to Mexico City, how long had she lived at the garbage dump, and what she hoped for in the future. I didn't have the heart to ask her to show us her most valuable item. But as I thanked her at the end of the interview, I heard over my shoulder, "Please, Señora, what is the most valuable thing you own?"

She looked at the producer. She looked at me. She dropped her eyes to her lap for a second and then, raising her head again, she surveyed her sorry surroundings. At last, she straightened, and said to him, "Mi familia."

Repeating it, this time looking into my eyes, she said, "Mi familia."

## Lonely

I miss Teddy. I miss eating together in the tiny kitchen in Mexico, and walking to see the cactus people. I miss praying with her. Or that's what I think I miss. I'm not self-aware enough to know that what I am longing for is someone to pay attention to me the way Teddy did. Back in Seattle, a day comes when I feel too lonely to stand.

There is a table in the kitchen where clean laundry is piled until it can be folded and sorted, which never happens. If someone's looking for a pair of socks or a clean shirt, they rummage through the pile until they find something.

I am in front of the table of clothes, searching for something to wear, when I give up. Dropping down to sit on the floor, I study the underside of my feet. I roll over and look up at the underside of the table. Hearing someone else coming to look for clothes, I scoot under the table to get out of the way, and whoever it is doesn't notice me.

After a while, I wonder why no one is looking for me. Now and then, I get up and go to the bathroom, or look for something to eat, and then I return to my spot under the laundry table. Carla's

145

legs race past in one direction, then Lotta's in another. John's sneakers appear as he searches for some item of clothing on the table. Later, Baby's legs go by. *Maybe she's looking for me*, I think with guilt, but don't say anything, not even to Baby. I become sore and cold from sitting on the hard linoleum floor, but stubbornness makes me endure it because now I'm determined to stay there until someone notices. I'm waiting for someone to say, "Hey, what's wrong with Hattie?"

When it gets dark, I go upstairs and go to bed. The next day I sit under the laundry table once more. I do it for three days. Nobody asks me why.

Not long afterward, in the upstairs bathroom, I pull open the little mirror above the sink to reveal the tiny medicine cabinet. Nothing looks interesting as I poke among things. I pick up Dad's razor and absentmindedly begin twisting the handle, watching the twin doors open and close.

Remembering that I heard once that people kill themselves by cutting their wrists, I carefully remove the blade to study it. It is rusty. Holding it carefully in my right hand so I won't cut myself, I gingerly test the blade by tapping my left finger against it. It is dull.

I decide to see if it will cut my wrist, tenderly at first, in case it hurts. That swipe only leaves a red mark, which is probably rust, I think, so I do it again a little harder. Nothing happens. I begin rubbing the edge back and forth across my left wrist, pressing against the skin to draw a bit of blood.

About then, an odd sensation overcomes me. I get a *picture* of myself, as if I can see me standing there in the small bathroom: dirty clothes pushed into every corner, stained sink with tiny pieces of soap next to the faucet, multiple brown rings in the never-washed tub with empty shampoo bottles cluttering its edge, and a disheveled twelve-year-old trying to slice her wrist with a rusty, dull blade. The image of it stops me. Shaken, I put the blade back into the razor and twist the handle, witnessing the twin doors descend.

I begin adopting myself out, like I run my own foster care agency. First up is Rena. She is the mom of Lilly's boyfriend. Diminutive and ladylike, Rena wears little white gloves and small round hats with a hint of veil above her brow. Her look would be regal but for the bent legs. Rena, I learn, had polio when she was my age and it left both legs twisted to the side and frozen in place. She is sitting when we first meet, so I don't see the legs until she stands and sets her gloved hand on my shoulder for stability. That touch makes me hers.

Rena works downtown in a dingy hotel above the Pike Place Market, changing sheets and sweeping. I help her. Rena grasps my elbow and rocks in her zigzag way along the narrow hallways as we go from room to room. When the work is finished, we descend an enclosed wooden staircase, her hand gripping me for balance. At the bottom of the stairs, she leans against the heavy door, pushing it open to reveal the colors and sounds of the market. We are Dorothy and Toto, suddenly in Oz.

Rena buys fresh strawberries from an impossibly bright fruit stand. We enter a closet-sized butcher shop and leave with a small bundle wrapped in white paper, its contents unknown to me because I can't pay attention to the words that are spoken. My eyes are too busy with the overwhelming sights. Into the current of people we go again, edging past giant fish on ice, their eyes staring up at me, past perfectly stacked carrots and brilliant green peppers, past the neon sign promising lunch with a view and past the man playing a guitar and singing as if anyone were listening. I am in the middle of it all, the girl at the market who is helping the lady do her shopping.

Back in her two-room apartment, Rena teaches me to make pork adobo, the favorite dish of her Filipino husband. He emerges from the back room with a nod, silently dishes out a plate, and disappears again. Rena pours us tea and begins another of her stories.

I always lose track of the tales, lulled by her soft voice with its slight accent. She is from a tribe in Canada and attended boarding schools that must have been British. There is something about her that makes me think of royalty. I try to copy the way she holds a teacup.

"More tea?" she asks.

"Yes, please."

If she is a queen, I am a princess. Though I never live with Rena, I visit her almost every week for eight months, maybe a year. Until Mrs. Saludo shows up.

"Who do you have here?" Mrs. Saludo bellows, as I hand Rena a paper plate of salmon. We are at a special picnic put on by the American Indian Women's Service League, an organization formed to help families like mine. There is salmon, salad, fry bread, and watermelon slices. Below the picnic tables, kids are running and playing on the sand. I am tempted to join them, but instead I am being Rena's princess, bringing her food, and now Mrs. Saludo is sizing me up.

"Who's this little one?" she asks.

Rena introduces us.

Mrs. Saludo is short and brown, with a belly that bobs along with her hearty laugh. Her mischievous eyes promise fun.

"Hello, little one. Get me a plate too?"

That simple request, without Rena or even me realizing it, is how Mrs. Saludo steals me away. She lives in Georgetown, the smokestack-riddled industrial part of Seattle, but you'd never know it when you swing open the gate in front of her house. It is a miniature farm.

"See these eyes?" Mrs. Saludo points to a dark speck on the potato in her hand. "You cut the potato into pieces so there is an eye on each piece. Like this, see?"

She is teaching me how to grow vegetables.

"You plant the eyes, little one. Plant the eyes."

She has rows of corn and towers of tomatoes. Beans climb up poles and squash plants snake underfoot.

At the end of summer, when the vegetables are done, Mrs. Saludo teaches me indoor things, like how to knit or how to do Indian beadwork. Most days now, after school, I catch a bus to Georgetown. Sometimes I feel guilty about dropping Rena, but at least I never bump into her so I don't have to see an abandoned look on her face. I do see one on Mom's, though, and it surprises me.

Mom makes a comment about me running off with Rena and Mrs. Saludo, so I decide to stay home more. I cook pork adobo for my own family. And try to plant a potato eye in the backyard, but it doesn't take. I would have maintained my resolve to stay at the house more, but then I catch sight of a boy: black-haired, twinkly eyed Sonny.

# Chapter 19

It was Oscar weekend, when all of Los Angeles gets swept up in the crowning of Hollywood royalty. I'd always found the star worship a tedious ritual, but this time I welcomed the distraction. The network had rented a suite above the Kodak Theater as a kind of "headquarters" for covering the show.

"We don't need the room until Sunday night, but we had to rent it for the whole weekend," the senior producer began, delicately.

I hoped the anticipation in my face wasn't too obvious.

"You could use it Friday and Saturday, if you wanted," she finished.

"Thank you. Thank you."

She knew I had slept in my office, was poaching friends' couches, and occasionally blowing money on expensive resorts and spas.

"Thank you," I said again, taking the key from her hand.

Hollywood and Vine was choked with tourists, TV crews, star managers, security officers, and street people all converging for the countdown to the Oscars. None of it mattered to me.

I slept in, relishing the simple act of lying in bed rather than sneaking out before dawn. The hotel room felt like a hospital room, a healing place. I didn't leave the room except for a short walk in the morning to buy food. Even then, I sauntered dreamily.

Upon my return, I sat down on the small sofa and peacefully surveyed my sanctuary. I'd been so distraught during the past four months that quieting my mind had often been impossible. I took deep, slow breaths, and relaxed. When an anxious thought began to form, I recognized it and let it go, returning again to focus on my breathing. Eventually, my eyes closed and the anxious thoughts came less frequently. I began to feel peaceful. Colors flashed on the inside of my eyelids: magenta, purple, a bit of orange. I grew more still.

Just as I began to come out of my meditation, with my eyes still closed, I felt a palpable sensation of a hand touching the top right side of my head, the way a parent might touch a child in tender love. The warm pressure of the hand upon my hair cupped me just above my right temple. It was lovely and so real that I opened my eyes to see whose hand it might be. As I did so, the "hand" lifted. I sat, blinking. *Something* had just happened. I felt I'd been blessed in some way. Whatever it was, I knew I wanted more of it.

I got off the couch and walked over to the bed, mystified. I lay back and fell into a two-hour nap.

The next morning, still marveling at the experience—and half not trusting it had been real—I tried to make it happen again. I repeated everything I had done the day before: took a walk, came back, sat on the sofa, breathed deeply, let go of thoughts, relaxed. Though I eventually became still, I couldn't shake the expectancy. I kept anticipating the touch. I waited for it, hungered for it, but it didn't come.

Just as I was giving up and opened my eyes, church bells began ringing.

I sprang from my seat and rushed to the window. Nine stories below, I saw people entering a church across the street.

I dashed to the closet for a dress and shoes. Without thinking, I moved as fast as I could out through the lobby and across the street to the church. Outside of an occasional Christmas or Easter service, I hadn't been to church in decades. I took a seat on a pew in the back.

Suddenly self-conscious, I wondered what drew me there. Someone up front was speaking, but the voice was simply background noise as I stared up at the image of Jesus in the stained-glass window high above the pulpit. When the choir sang, I felt transported.

As the service ended people began filing out, but I remained motionless, still captivated by the music echoing in the cavernous space.

A few people, rather than leaving, were headed up the center aisle in twos and threes. I felt compelled to follow them. As they neared the front of the church they formed a semicircle of about twelve people. I couldn't see over the shoulders ahead of me so I didn't know why they did this. I made my way to the left to join the semicircle, and that's when I saw the preacher in his long white robe, handing out bread and wine.

*Communion.*

Hesitation gripped me. I hadn't taken communion since I was about eight years old, at church with Aunt Teddy.

*Can I do this? What does it mean? Am I making a commitment?*

The bread and wine were before me. I closed my eyes and opened my mouth, vaguely hearing the preacher say: "The body and blood of Jesus Christ, broken and shed for you . . ."

Nothing happened. No bolt from the sky tore through the place. I opened my eyes to see the semicircle break up, with most of the people heading out of the church. As I turned to leave, I caught a glimpse of a few of them headed in the opposite direction, toward the front of the church again.

Once more, I followed them. There were only about four or five in the group now. I felt I needed to be with them. In front of the altar was a low, velvet railing. They knelt upon it. I copied them. They bent their heads in prayer. I bent mine. A tiny part of me wondered what I was doing, but a greater part kept me in place.

With my head bowed, I remembered all the prayers I had written in the journal by my bedside since reading Isaiah 54.

*Let God be your husband . . .*

Just then, I heard murmuring and peeked to see that the preacher stood before the kneelers to my right. He seemed to be coming down the row, praying for each. I closed my eyes and waited.

When he reached me, my mind was empty of prayer. I was nothing more than a wounded woman, a vacant vessel, kneeling in a church with no idea why.

I felt warm oil touch my forehead, as his finger made the sign of the cross.

*He anointeth my head with oil.*

I strained to hear, but could not make out the words of the minister's whispered blessing. Then, it happened.

The touch of his hand cupped the top right side of my head. The warmth, the pressure, the duration were exactly what I'd felt the day before. The invisible had become real, here in the house of God.

I opened my eyes, in awe.

*God, you are real.*

I soared out of the sanctuary lighter than I had ever been. My joy could not be contained. It was as if I were a different person—no longer uncertain about what life might hold for me because of the divorce. In fact, the divorce was so miniscule a thing that it hardly registered. I skipped back to the hotel full of a magnificent, gigantic love, one that came from God, a God who would, and had, reached out and touched me.

A revolution of mind—no—of soul had taken place, changing every external and internal perspective. It was more than I could at first comprehend. There was an immediate sense that I need never fear anything or anyone, ever. That alone was overwhelming, but more than a sense of being protected and loved, there followed the astonishing conviction that I had been sought out for this love.

God had called me with his touch.

Riding the elevator back to my room, I admitted that what had happened was beyond my limited conception of God. At times in life, I may have had a vague notion of God out there somewhere, but there was nothing vague about this experience. The touch upon my head had been tangible—a physical experience. It had led me into a church, a Christian church, where the touch had been confirmed. I walked with certainty while my spirit did cartwheels.

Teddy was right.

"He restoreth my soul," she taught me.

*Oh, Aunt Teddy, you were right. God does restore.*

*Restore*, said each footstep as I walked the hallway to my room, *restore.*

*But wait*, I thought, *it's one thing to believe in God restoring, but Jesus? Did the touch mean I was now to follow Jesus?* Of course, it did. The touch led me to a *Christian* church. Jesus is *Christ*. Jesus had called me to him. Jesus. Christ.

I had no idea what it meant to really follow Jesus. I remembered reading about him with Aunt Teddy, but couldn't recall all the stories. There was walking on water, and . . . what else?

My mind reeled.

True, I'd been reading the Bible, but mostly the Old Testament: Isaiah, Psalms, and Proverbs. Jesus wasn't mentioned there, was he? I raced back to the room to check a Gideon Bible, but upon arriving I encountered producers hauling in gear. Oscar night was only hours away, and they needed the hotel suite.

I could barely focus on packing up my things and getting ready for that night's job of covering the Oscar parties. I still had to pull the all-nighter that the assignment required, but none of those tasks mattered. I was detached from the intensity of everyone around me, the actors and their handlers, the cameramen and photographers pushing each other to get a shot. None of it bothered me, not even the hyper producer who normally stressed out everyone around her. It felt like I was floating above it all, thinking about

God's touch. I didn't feel a flicker of weariness or tension, nor did I think about my divorce.

My life had changed.

Contentment encircled me.

On the red carpet, I suddenly remembered Teddy teaching me the song, "Jesus loves me, this I know," and laughed aloud, causing the nervous producer to give me a stern look and a "Shhh."

Lined up with the other reporters who hoped to get sound bites from the night's winners, I was a middle-aged woman who felt like a little girl in Sunday school, a true believer singing at the top of her lungs.

# Chapter 20

"Fire!"

Mom's eyes are wild, her thin body astoundingly strong as she leaps up the steps two at a time, calling her warning.

"Get out, get out! The house is on fire!"

She is fierce in herding us. We flop out of bed, spill past her in a charge down the staircase, out the front door, all the way down the seventeen concrete steps to the street. She won't follow until everyone is out. Until everyone is safe.

Mom, the mighty, didn't choose this haunted house. She was in the hospital with her lupus when we moved. She told Dad, "Choose anything, as long as it doesn't have steps." And now, here she is, a wonder woman saving us from his crazy choice.

Mom . . . Mom . . .

White-capped rapids roiled in the normally placid river below. I steered carefully along the twisting road, bound for my cabin.

*Can I handle this?*

Forested mountains ascended to my left. A low-angled sun cast a glare upon the swollen river just as a deer darted across the highway. I slowed, gripping the wheel of my pickup truck.

*Yes, I can. I am ready for this.*

After the touch upon my head, and the conviction that God was real and loved me, I felt empowered not just spiritually but emotionally and physically. This task, which I had previously avoided, was now upon me. The Forest Service road climbed away from the river. A logging road branched off to the right. I took the lower fork, descending to follow a twisting creek that flowed out of the mountains. I rolled down the window to listen to its rushing and to breathe in the evening air.

*I am home.*

Turning off the engine, I was greeted by the outright silence of a Montana forest. An almost-full moon lit the steps to the cabin.

*Why did I stay away so long?*

With a shove of the door, I was inside my cabin for the first time in seven months. It was cold, and there was no kindling by the woodstove. Despite the chill, I didn't rush to gather wood. I walked from room to room, my hand tracing the log walls. My footsteps left no echo to announce my presence. But I was there, in my own safe place. That thought reminded me I had a job to do.

I trotted down to the basement storeroom for boxes. Maybe I couldn't get him out of my house, but I could at least get his stuff out of my cabin. I recognized this for what it was, displaced energy and frustration, but I let the cathartic work have its way with me. Into the first box, I put his T-shirts. Underwear and socks took up the next. Each box I filled renewed me. I grew lighter as they grew heavier. I kept at it until well after midnight, when I began to shake with the cold, then I crawled into bed.

Sunlight skimming the top of Cougar Mountain woke me. Rolling over, I looked out the loft window and spotted a coyote dashing across the gravel drive. I laid back and gazed up at the cedar plank ceiling, high overhead. Everything my eyes took in was medicine.

*Why had I ever stayed away?*

I got up and kneeled in prayer.

"Dear God, thank you for bringing me home."

In the kitchen, as I made hot water for tea, I stopped to recognize that each movement was a gift. It had been months since I could move freely in any kitchen, preparing breakfast for myself. Appreciating the luxury of it, I set my bowl on the table and sat to enjoy my simple meal. I didn't have to dash out the back door or eat in my car.

I felt a deep compassion for myself, and lingered at the table. Outside, the national forest stretched for miles. A thin mist floated above the creek. From where I sat, there was no evidence of other human beings, no car or house to mar the view.

Eventually, I returned to packing up his things.

"You should give it all to Goodwill," one friend had advised me.

"Why don't you throw his stuff away?" Jeanie had asked.

When the bedroom closet was finally empty, I turned to the back mudroom for his hats, gloves, and coats. In the basement were cowboy boots and hunting gear. In the bathroom, I was startled at the sight of his hair clinging to a brush.

A knock at the door made me jump.

"Let us in," my sisters' voices bellowed through the door. Jo Ann and Lilly stood there, smiling and shivering, when I swung open the door. Not wanting me to be alone, they'd driven hours across the mountains. I could barely contain my gratitude. We easily slipped into sibling banter. No one mentioned the fifteen boxes stacked against the wall.

When we walked about the property, Lilly advised burning the matted, dead grass. "Remember when Grandpa used to do that?"

As little girls visiting Idaho in the springtime, we'd watched him burn the fields of dead weeds and grass that surrounded his small house on the reservation. Once the snow had completely melted, he turned the ground smoky and black.

"Reduces the fire danger," Lilly went on. "All this undergrowth should be burned."

Our feet crunched over dead trumpet ferns and withered knapweed clumped on a carpet of pine needles several inches deep. All of it was damp, but by August it would be a tinder-dry bed of kindling, leading right up to my log cabin.

"Hmm," I considered. "I've never tried something like that before."

Jo Ann threw a lit match on the ground. It quickly went out.

"We'll need more than that," she said.

Soon we had a propane torch in hand, igniting circles of flame that spread two or three feet before dying out on their own.

"The grass is too wet," Lilly said. "It needs a couple days of sun."

With that, we returned inside where Jo Ann, determined to see something burn, stoked a blaze to life in the fireplace. I put a pot of stew on the table and promised my sisters a homemade huckleberry pie like Grandma used to make.

Later, in our bathing suits, the three of us squealed as we dashed across patches of snow to the hot springs. The air was freezing, but the water was over a hundred degrees. Through the rising mist from the pools, stars sparkled in the black Montana sky. I looked at my loved ones and felt elevated, lifted high above life's sorrows. Spontaneously, I climbed out of the steamy water, ran across the snow, and plunged into the cold water pool, emerging with shrieks of joy.

After my sisters' noisy departure the next morning, full of laughter and hugs, I was left alone with the boxes. I carried them out, one by one. After fifteen trips up and down the back stairs, I finally had his stuff out of my cabin. Next, it was a drive to a small town, where I ferried the boxes from my truck into a shop that agreed to ship them. I wrote his office address on the label, and at last I was done.

It was dark by the time I got back to the cabin. Tired but pleased, I climbed up to my bed in the loft and fell asleep to a coyote's call.

The phone woke me. In the pitch black, I was momentarily confused. The phone rang again, clanging against the silence.

"Hello?" I croaked sleepily.

Silence.

"Hello?"

Silence.

The silent calls had begun about a month earlier. In Los Angeles they were irritating, but here the call felt ominous. I was alone in a forest, miles from the nearest town. My heart beat rapidly as I set down the receiver. It was stupid to come to Montana alone.

I lay awake in the dark, afraid that I might see headlights appear on the road to my cabin. The coyotes had moved on. There was no sound. As the minutes stretched to hours, I became convinced it was a wrong number. I was safe. After a time, I drifted back to sleep.

Tap. Tap. Tap.

I bolted up. It was dawn.

*Was I dreaming?*

I peered down from the loft window to see if someone might be at the back door: no one. I glided softly down the stairs to the main floor to check the side door: no one.

Tap. Tap. Tap.

*It's coming from the basement.*

I tiptoed down the basement stairs, all of my senses sharp.

Tap. Tap.

*Someone's trying to break in!*

I paused before descending to the bottom step.

Tap . . . Tap. Tap.

The sound was right around the corner.

Tap. Tap.

I took a deep breath and peeked around the corner.

The wild turkey's head snapped back. Four of them danced about on the other side of the window, the splash of red at their necks bright against their dirty grey bodies. The biggest one attacked his reflection in the glass.

Tap. Tap. Tap.

*Wildlife.*

I sagged against the wall. At my movement, the turkeys scattered, looking as terrified as I had felt. I began to laugh at their fear and mine, letting my laughter grow until I shook.

*Am I getting daffy? No, you are jumpy. And jumpy isn't such an odd thing to be, under the circumstances.*

I dressed, and walked out to find the ground less frosty than it had been the day before. Too timid to use the propane torch without my sisters around, I tried lighting a match to see if the grass might catch. It flickered only briefly before dying, leaving a tiny black circle at my feet.

The most dangerous part of my property was the hillside below my cabin. If someone drove by and tossed a cigarette, that would be the place. A grass fire could ignite and burn right up the hill to the cabin. My sisters were right. I needed a preemptive burn to get rid of all the pine needles and dead, dry ferns.

In the cold, clear morning, I stood at the top of the hill. My plan was to burn a line across the top, then descend a few feet and light a fire that would burn up to the blackened line, where it would naturally extinguish. I planned to repeat those steps until the entire hillside was burned—a buffer against fire, a way to feel safer. But after an hour, all I had were twenty small black circles, no more than five inches in diameter. My fingers were freezing.

I returned to the house, crunching over dead ferns, for another box of matches. Again, I dropped matches along the hillside, and this time the circles grew seven to ten inches before dying.

*This is ridiculous.*

I sat on the ground, listening to the creek. I don't know how much time passed. It was easy to lose myself listening to water race over rocks. After a time, as I fingered the dead grass, I realized it felt drier than it had earlier. A slight breeze brushed my face. I closed my eyes to enjoy it.

*Get back to work.*

I lit another match, and another. The circles joined before turning upward to my "stop" line. Encouraged, I dropped down the slope an extra four or five feet more and lit ten matches, dropping them in a row across the hillside. The circles of flame quickly united. The fire was alive.

It was gratifying to see the black carpet grow as the head of the fire burned upward. My system was working.

My pleasure, however, was short lived. I discovered fire does not behave as expected. Instead of burning only upward, a ribbon of flame turned sideways, moving toward a grove of evergreens. I scrambled up the slope to grab my loppers and raced back down the hill.

I needed to cut off the lower branches so the tree wouldn't catch fire. I snipped as fast as I could, while keeping my eye on the approaching ground fire. The flames were only a foot high, although as they burned through the thick grass, they occasionally ignited long-buried stumps and then shot higher. I cut branches so fast that my arm muscles hurt. Then I saw the uselessness of my action. The branches tangled at my feet as the flames approached. I grabbed them and hurled them like javelins, as far from the flames as I could. The fire was four feet from me when I decided to stomp it out.

But fire is like liquid. It flows all around.

Even as my stomping feet extinguished a small area, more fire grew to my left and my right.

*I need a hose!*

I struggled up the vertical slope and sprinted around the far side of the cabin for the hose. It was heavy and tangled. As I worked to unwind it, I realized that I could no longer see what was happening on the hill. I recalled every forester's warning: never leave a fire unattended. Using all my strength, I pulled and stretched the hose around the front of the cabin. It barely reached the edge of my lawn, where the hill drops down to the road. I raced back to turn on the water, then ran again to the slope to begin spraying down toward the group of trees.

The fire had reached them but had not yet ignited them. It burned among the tree trunks where the needles were piled deeply. I soaked the area. Eventually columns of thick smoke rose and it seemed the crisis had passed.

That's when I looked over my shoulder.

On the far edge of the slope, toward the back of the cabin, flames were four feet high and speeding up the hill toward the six-hundred-gallon propane tank.

*Do I run away? No, I have to run toward it, to try to stop it.*

I sped across the hillside, jumping over burning stumps, slipping on the blackened ground, running toward the inferno. The fire was fueled by logging slash, debris left by the loggers who'd cleared the property fifteen years earlier. It was eager to burn. I grabbed pieces of wood ten feet long and thicker than a man's arm. I threw them as far as my declining strength would allow.

Dashing to a spot just downhill of the tank, I tossed dead branches and logs while nervously watching the tongues of flame lick wildly into the air below me. They were too tall for stomping out.

*The hose. You need the hose.*

My heavy feet were barely cooperative as I willed myself up the steep hill one more time. I ran to the front of the cabin and pulled on the hose. It wouldn't reach. I needed to drag it all the way back around the blind side of the cabin in order for it to reach the propane tank. A hundred feet of hose never felt heavier. My legs and arms were on the edge of giving out.

*Dear God, please help me.*

When I finally made it around the cabin and back to the propane tank, I saw that a shift in wind had saved me. The fire had turned away from the tank and was now burning in a downhill direction. *Doesn't fire always burn uphill?* I thought dully, as I drenched the ground around the propane tank.

*Thank you, God.*

As abruptly as it had arisen, the wind died. What had begun as "a little black circle" was now a jagged-edged area seventy feet long and at least that wide—and still growing, though more slowly. I stumbled down the hill to stamp out the smoldering edges. Though no longer roaring, they were headed toward another stand of trees. At any moment, a burst of wind could whip up the fire. It took me forty-five minutes of stomping and kicking at the ground before I made my way full-circle around the burn. Exhausted, I plopped down in the midst of the moonscape.

Plumes of smoke surrounded me. Everywhere, the ground was grey-white with streaks of black. An occasional flash of orange caught my eye from the dozens of stumps within the black circle that were still burning. The air was filled with ash. My senses slowed, as if my mind were as depleted as my body.

Out of nowhere came a popping sound. I turned my head to witness a thirty-foot pine suddenly ignite, its needles crackling from the ground to the tip of its crown. There was nothing I could do. I held my breath as the tree, standing in the center of the blackened hill, became a torch almost three stories high. If the wind blew, it would ignite other trees and could burn my cabin.

*God, please let there be no wind.*

The tall pine's needles were gone in seconds. They burned themselves out, leaving a black skeleton reaching for the sky. I exhaled, and collapsed backward onto the ground, not caring that my hair was lying in ash. I was so exhausted I wanted to sleep right there. Perhaps that was the effect of smoke inhalation.

I didn't have enough energy to laugh at myself. I couldn't even lift my head. I stared straight up, catching a glimpse of blue sky, between wisps of grey smoke. The fire was so clearly a metaphor of how my life felt—barely controlled, on the verge of disaster, terrifying, exhausting, beyond my ability to manage. But as I thought about it, I realized that the more the idea of God had consumed my thoughts in these weeks and months, the more my perspective had shifted.

Maybe the burn didn't represent the chaos and tragedy of an incinerated marriage and a forsaken middle-aged woman, but rather it reflected the way God was slowly consuming my life and heart. I sat up and recognized the necessity, the good, of the scorched landscape. The burn had cleared out things that needed to go. It created a hedge of safety and the promise of new growth, new life. And it seemed the fire knew its boundaries—I could trust the purifying flames to go just far enough and no further.

# Chapter 21

Dad has a hobby, now. He calls himself a "rock hound." It makes me laugh inside that his hobby has the word "hound" in it, since Mom's illness means "wolf." It's like they were meant for each other.

I love his new hobby. We all do. Because being a rock hound means digging for rocks. And you don't do that in the city. Being a rock hound means packing the car up with all of us and heading out to creek beds, or to forested slopes where agates might be. It means we kids can run wild in the woods and maybe splash in the water. It means a picnic, one of our favorite things, if Mom is along to build a small fire where we can roast hot dogs. It means tired rides home, full of contentment.

## What's Your Name?

I thought about those rock hunting trips after another sisters' get-together. This one had been a milestone birthday celebration, which seemed to be happening frequently. Since there were six of us getting up in years, someone was always turning fifty, fifty-five, or sixty. At this lunch, with its usual razzing and reminiscing, one of them had brought up the "road sign Indian names."

"What?" I asked.

"Don't you remember? We all had names based on road signs."

"All except Carlotta." Jo Ann chuckled. "She insisted on being called Running Bear even though we told her that's not a road sign."

I didn't remember. And my lack of recollection mystified me. "Where were we? How did it happen?"

No one could recall the details, only the names, which they repeated at each other, pointing and laughing so hard they had to wipe away tears. I wondered how I could have forgotten a day so gleeful that it still tickled them decades later.

"Did I have a road sign name?" I asked, and got only shrugs in reply. If I had one, they couldn't remember it. Maybe I'd been away that day, off somewhere with Rena or Mrs. Saludo. But I didn't like the thought that I'd missed out on such fun.

Travelling home from that birthday lunch, I let myself imagine the Indian naming day. I pictured us in the car on our way home from rock hunting. We're deliriously exhausted and singing silly songs when we tumble into naming ourselves. A popular song from the radio is in the air, its lyrics capturing us, "Running Bear loves Little White Dove . . ."

"I'm Running Bear," Lotta announces, which makes us fall upon her.

"You can't be Running Bear. Running Bear is a boy."

"He is not."

"Is too."

"White Dove is the girl. Running Bear is the boy."

"Her name is *Little* White Dove, stupid."

The older ones, John and Lilly, who've recently started powwow dancing and therefore would know about Indian names, give our dispute a moment's consideration before agreeing that Running Bear would make a fine Indian name.

We are a bunch of half-native kids who've been playing in the woods all day, crammed into a car on a winding, forested road, pondering for the first time in our lives what our Indian names might be. Carla, distracted, or maybe frightened, by the image on a yellow road sign up ahead asks, "Dad, what does that sign say?"

"Falling Rocks," he answers.

"That's my Indian name," she declares.

Everyone hoots.

"You can't be Falling Rocks."

"I can too. And I am. I'm Falling Rocks!" Her enlarging eyes and quivering lip let us know she's serious.

"OK, OK. You're Falling Rocks."

Mom turns to smile at us over her shoulder.

"Baby gets the next one," she says, which makes all of us peer ahead to see what name awaits Baby. After a couple more bends in the road, there it is.

"That's me. What does it say? What's my name?"

"Deer on the Highway." John laughs aloud, along with Mom, Dad, and Lilly.

Running Bear, Falling Rocks, and Deer on the Highway are so pleased that they can't sit still. They bounce on their knees on the backseat, clasping hands and grinning at each other. Watching them, I neglect to keep a look out for the next yellow road sign bearing a name. Annie gets it.

"Bingo!" she blares. "There I am!"

The big people bellow in laughter, but because the sign has already zipped past, I have no idea what happened or why it's funny.

"What? What was it? What's your name?"

"Just call me: Caution, Soft Shoulder." She nods.

"Let me see, is your shoulder soft?" Lilly teases.

We are a car full of giggles: Dad with his arm around Mom, the three oldest, the three youngest. Determined to get in on the fun, I scan for road signs ahead, but by now the twisting two-lane road is joining the highway that runs like a straight, wide ribbon right into Seattle. I don't want to be Yield or Lane Ending or Merge Left.

After a while, I give up searching for an Indian name and gradually return my attention to our world inside the car.

Falling Rocks is falling asleep. Deer on the Highway is sucking her thumb.

Soft Shoulder is smiling as she gazes out the side window, her fingers tapping to a tune she is humming to herself, something I can't quite make out. Maybe it's Running Bear loves Little White Dove.

## Homebound

Returning to Los Angeles from my cabin, I felt compelled to go to church, but wasn't sure where. It was no longer enough to simply pray "God, help me" and, "Thanks for the help, God." The touch on my head had been real, and it had been confirmed when I walked into a Christian church. Therefore, I wanted to learn what it meant to be a Christian. Though Jeanie had directed me to Isaiah 54, she did not belong to a church. I realized I didn't know any churchgoing Christians.

*Wait a minute, there was one who used to work in the LA news bureau. I could call her, but what do I say? "Hi, I felt God's touch upon my head. And God saved my cabin by changing the wind direction, and I thought I'd call . . ."*

I decided against a phone call, but on the Thursday before Easter I sent a restrained email: "Hi, how are you? I was just wondering, do you have a recommendation for a Good Friday service?" I don't know why I stopped there and didn't ask about Easter. I mean, if you're going to inquire about church, why not go all the way?

Good Friday arrived before I received a response. Driving home from work, I saw a sign outside a church announcing services at 8 p.m. I pulled over and sat in my car until people began to gather in front of Saint Albans Church, near UCLA.

We were each handed a candle and, in a procession, carried them into the darkened sanctuary. There was singing and prayer. But I didn't introduce myself to anyone and when it was over I drove home, uncertain what it had all meant.

On Saturday, a woman from the salsa dance class at the gym asked if I'd like to join her and her family at the Hollywood Bowl Easter service.

"Really? They have Easter at the Hollywood Bowl?"

"Yes, there's a sunrise service. But we're going to the later service at 11 a.m."

"I never knew there was Easter at the Hollywood Bowl. Yes. I'd love to go with you."

This person had never invited me to anything before, but there we were arranging a meeting time and place, and the next day I joined her family in a box at the Hollywood Bowl.

With the choir's last song still reverberating, the pastor issued the invitation. Anyone seeking prayer was welcome to come to the front. I mumbled something to excuse myself from the box and moved forward with a stilted gait. Though I heartily wanted prayer, my legs seemed to argue against the long walk down the center aisle. "Anyone seeking prayer . . ." that would be me, and yet my steps were tentative.

A tall woman with wispy red hair looked earnestly into my eyes.

"My husband of seventeen years," I stammered, "said he just settled for me . . ." Would it be wrong to ask her to call down his damnation? That wasn't what had propelled me forward, I thought, stopping myself. That wasn't the prayer I was seeking. This was about me, not him. I was standing there because more than a month earlier I'd felt a touch on my head and I was confused about what to do with that experience.

"I need prayer because . . . I don't know what my life is supposed to be."

It seemed impossible to describe all that had fallen apart—or was it all that had fallen into place?

"What's your name?" she asked, taking my hands into hers.

"Hattie," I stammered, distracted by the feel of her soft, cool palms. I saw that her eyes were a light greenish brown. A few freckles decorated the bridge of her nose.

"Well, Hattie," she said, "let's give it to the Lord."

*That's it,* I wanted to exclaim, *that's what I want to find out. How do you give things to the Lord?* But I couldn't ask, because she'd already launched into prayer.

"Dear heavenly Father . . ."

Belatedly, I closed my eyes and bowed my head.

"We ask your blessing upon Hattie. Heal her pain, Lord. Help her to see that you are all that she needs. Carry her through this time, Father God. Just hold her, let her feel your presence."

As the prayer went on, I became lost in the cadence of her words and in my tears. I gripped her hands tightly, and shut my eyes against the spectacle we must have presented. In the back of my mind came a brief shame that I was standing in public, praying with a stranger, but that sense lost itself in my gratitude for her every word. When it was over, I walked away in exhausted relief.

Later that night, as I laid in bed, I was aghast that I'd gotten up to pray at the Hollywood Bowl.

*People will think I'm crazy if they ever find out I'm doing this. Can Indians be willing Christians? After all, the missionaries were forced on us. On top of that, you're a news reporter. Are news correspondents allowed to believe in God?*

I did a quick review of the correspondents I knew and couldn't come up with any professed Christians. I recalled the time a correspondent in the Chicago Bureau had used the phrase "The Lord" in a story, referring to a flood-ravaged community relying upon the Lord, and a producer had complained that it was an inappropriate thing to say on air.

*And here I am, believing God speaks to me through verses in the Bible, and asking for prayer from a complete stranger . . . at the Hollywood Bowl, no less.*

# Chapter 22

Wind whips my hair left and right, stinging my forehead. I turn to see if my sisters' long brown hair is caught up in the dusty wind like mine. But looking to the side only blinds me as my locks fly over my face. We laugh against the onslaught and hold tight to the top of the cab.

We are standing up in the back of the pickup truck, a line of heads peeking over the cab, as it rises and descends the rolling hills of the prairie. Undulating fields of green stretch to the right and left of us, and straight ahead is the gravel ribbon of road rising up and down until it disappears.

The wind, the sun, and our destination make us giddy beyond words. We are on our way to Talmaks, where our grandparents camp for two weeks every summer. We don't always get to go with them, and rarely stay the entire time, but any day at Talmaks is a gift immeasurable to us. Life is abundant and full at Talmaks. Joy lives here.

The pickup truck slows and turns onto an intersecting gravel road, not visible until we're right upon it. I wonder how they know where to turn. This new gravel strip between the fields is identical to the last, a gentle roller coaster which carries us: two old people in the cab, seven shrieking kids in the back, and a cloud of dust following behind.

"There's the little house," John calls out over the wind.

Up ahead we see the tiny house at the edge of the woods. It's a sign that Talmaks is near. By tradition, we can't begin chanting until we pass the little house. Zipping past it, we begin, "Yay, Yay for Talmaks. Yay, Yay for Talmaks."

The pickup slows for another turn, and suddenly the forested hill of Talmaks comes into sight.

"Yay, Yay for Talmaks."

Our chant drops to a whisper when we turn left onto the carpet of pine needles. Maybe it's because the tires aren't on gravel anymore and the hushed ground quiets us. Or maybe it's the feeling of being so small under the towering Ponderosa trees. Or maybe we're simply in awe.

We're here.

At Talmaks, we are a tumble of happy kids racing through the trees, gathering pinecones and downed branches for campfires. While our grandparents put up the tent, we spy other kids in other camps. Instantly, we play.

Grandpa chops kindling and Grandma gets the woodstove going while we dart about, free. After dinner, a bell will clang in the distance. A moment later it rings again, the sound resonating through the forest. Grandma throws a wool shawl over her shoulders and leaves us to walk to the church tent in the center of the grassy field. I wonder what pulls at her. Why does she drop everything when those bells ring? What or who calls to her when they chime? My grandmother seems no more at home anywhere than she does here at Talmaks, where the church bells ring. I long to know that kind of home.

## God Heals

I drove down the hill from our Brentwood home one day and saw a sign outside a church that said, "How God Heals Hurt." I pulled over. Walking through the doorway of the small brick church, I found myself going upstream against a flow of people exiting.

"Um, hi," I said to a man who had a kindly look about him. "I'm here because of the sign outside."

He smiled.

"You know the sign? How God Heals Hurt?" I paused uncertainly. He nodded.

"That's our special series. You just missed it."

"Missed it? I'm not going to learn how God heals hurt?"

"I'm sorry."

I drove away deflated.

Over the next weeks, I visited a variety of churches, sometimes in LA and often while on assignment in one city or another. The big screens with song lyrics scrolling along them, like in some karaoke bar, surprised me. When had church become a rock concert? I discovered that modern-day services were not like the ones I remembered from church with Teddy, where the choir wore robes and the pastor was somber. At first, I was taken aback at the raised hands and arm-waving of some worshipers. I dropped in on Catholic, Baptist, Assembly of God, Methodist, and Episcopalian congregations.

Bel Air Presbyterian Church, perched on a cliff in the Santa Monica Mountains, was the sixth church I'd visited since that February day when I'd felt the touch upon my head. Listening to the soprano's voice soar in the spacious sanctuary, I knew I'd finished searching.

"I really liked that service," I said idly to a white-haired woman who exited next to me.

We chatted for a few minutes about the church.

"Ronald Reagan used to worship here," she said.

"Really?"

That odd tidbit gave me a measure of how unrecognizable my life had become.

*What am I doing in Ronald Reagan's former church?*

Seeing the lost look on my face, she asked if I'd like to join her small prayer group.

"We meet every Tuesday night in Santa Monica."

I was momentarily without will, something she seemed to understand.

"I'll show you where. We could meet somewhere convenient and I could just lead you there. How about Ralph's grocery on Wilshire?"

Days later, I sat in my car with the motor off, watching people haul carts of groceries to their cars.

*This is ridiculous. That lady's probably not going to show up.*

But there she was, waving at me from the driver's seat of an SUV. She signaled for me to follow her, and pulled away from the supermarket.

"This is Hattie," she said when we had arrived, introducing me to the group.

Strangers stood to shake my hand. The setting was a small living room in a ground-floor apartment. Mismatched chairs had been pulled into a semicircle facing a low couch in the corner. I felt like I'd walked into the kind of scene a news crew might shoot for a story. "The New Christians," it would be called. "They meet in living rooms . . ." would begin my narration.

There were eight of us. The leader, a man in his forties, began to read from the book of Mark. In turn, each person spoke about what the passage meant to them. My ability to listen was clouded by relentless judging of the people, the room, and my presence in it. Though I was sitting on the couch, my back was erect and wouldn't rest against it.

"I really need a job," a young lady said, catching my attention. The time allotted for studying the book of Mark must have ended. They were going around the room now, requesting prayer for one thing or another. I didn't see anyone writing down these requests, and wondered how they would be transmitted to the pastor in the big church on the hill.

Someone asked for prayer for a sick relative. One guy wanted prayer for his dating life. That made me want to bolt the room, but just then I noticed they were all looking at me expectantly. It was my turn.

"Oh," I said. "Well . . . um, I've never been to a small group before. I just, I was hunting for a church, or something."

*Tell them about the hand that so tenderly touched you.*

But I couldn't. Instead, I stammered on.

"I believed in God when I was little but gave it up . . . and well, in this divorce . . . I mean, I'm still married, at least technically, but it's actually over because he . . ."

They looked at me with concern. I saw no judgment in their eyes.

". . . out of the blue one day, after seventeen years . . ."

I lost track of the room, letting my sentences spill out, whether coherent or not.

"I've been living like a refugee. I sleep in hotels, or with friends, or . . ."

At that, someone put a hand on my knee. The human touch broke through to me. I looked up and saw tears in the eyes of my listeners.

"Wait a minute. I know this story," said a redhead across the room. "I prayed for you! At the Hollywood Bowl, remember?"

Her features came into focus. Suddenly, we were both laughing at how unlikely it was that we would meet again. There had been hundreds, maybe thousands, of people at the Hollywood Bowl on Easter, and yet the tall woman with the freckles on her nose who had held my hands and prayed with me was sitting in the same Santa Monica living room months later.

"What are the odds?" I wondered aloud.

"Not odds. God," said the white-haired woman.

I smiled at her and felt myself, finally, lean back into the couch.

"Well, let's pray," said the leader.

One at a time, their voices were lifted, never presenting their own requests, but each praying for another. I felt my tears again, when a voice to the left said, "And Lord, we lift up Hattie . . ." Others murmured, "Yes, Lord, protect her."

We formed a circle of prayer, empathy, worship, and love. No one went unnoticed.

# Chapter 23

I'm thirteen when I get my first boyfriend. Though he flips it back, his black hair keeps falling over his dark, smiling eyes. He's standing with friends on the corner as our van pulls up. They shift nervously in their Levi jackets, their hands in their pockets, four skinny Indian boys.

Pretending not to look at them, I sit in the van with three other girls, on this, our first day of our first ever summer job.

"Dibs," I say, gesturing out the window at him, whose name I learn is Sonny.

"No, I dibs," says Phyllis.

*Yeah, like he'd go for you.*

The guys step into the van, to our shy smiles and stolen glances, and we drive off to the theater where we'll be paid a dollar sixty an hour to put on a play. None of us are actors. We're inner-city teenagers in a summer get-them-off-the-street government program.

By the end of that first day, on our ride home, Sonny sits next to me, our knees almost touching. We're alike. He has a white father and an Indian mother, just like me, and they drink too much, just like mine, and he has six siblings just like I do. By the end of the week, Sonny asks someone to buy us beer and he gives me a hickey.

In our house, drinking age is around thirteen. At least, that's what I figure. I convince myself that Mom let Lilly drink when she became a teenager and probably John too, although I never saw that. Annie was in Idaho, so who knows about her. At any rate, Sonny and I are off to the races.

One New Year's Day, I am fifteen and sitting on the floor at home nursing a bottle of Southern Comfort. On a sudden impulse, I stand up, wavering a bit, and in heavy concentration determine that what I really need is to see my boyfriend. I want Sonny. Right now.

Barefoot, and wearing a long, caftan hippie gown, I make my way out the front door, stumbling down the seventeen concrete steps to begin the two-mile walk to Sonny's. I don't feel my toes scraping the cement. I'm unaware of the blood on my feet or the January cold.

Crossing the Twelfth Street Bridge that connects Beacon Hill to Chinatown, a feeling comes over me. It's a desire to erase myself. I pause at the railing and look down at the cars far below.

Unsteadily, my raw feet climb over the metal rail, my red hands clinging to the green-painted steel. A car stops on the bridge. A lady gets out and begins talking to me, but in my drunkenness I understand only that she wants something. Why is she bothering me? I focus intently on her moving lips, trying to decipher her words, unconsciously leaning toward her, and that's when she grabs my elbows to support me as I crawl back over the railing to listen to her. She walks me across the bridge, talking, talking . . . I have no idea what about.

At the end of the bridge, I recognize through my haze a street name, King Street.

"My boyfriend lives here," I slur.

"Good," she says, steering me on. "Good."

## Inheritance

It is ironic, but not surprising, that children of alcoholics often become alcoholics. Even when they manage to escape the disease themselves, they will often unconsciously choose an alcoholic for a spouse.

John was the first to get sober, shocking us with news that he'd joined AA, since he, of all of us, never seemed to have a problem. John was the star, the one child that Mom and Dad got dressed up for and applauded at school plays. He'd become a successful actor and director in Seattle, and I was a news reporter and anchor. It was around this time when he called to say he wanted to come over to talk to me about drinking.

*No thanks*, I thought, and left the house. When I got home later that night I saw that he'd left an AA Big Book leaning against my doorstep. I never asked him if the drinking problem he wanted to talk about that day was his, or possibly mine. I wasn't ready to hear.

One sign of alcoholism is personality change—the Jekyll and Hyde phenomenon. It hit me immediately. I'd be laughing hilariously one second and the next turning a murderous glare at my teenage boyfriend, the same kind Mom gave Dad. The look that says, "I'm going to claw your eyes out."

## Sonny

Sonny and I are a combustible combination. Like me, he acts out the drinking and fighting he's grown up with. When I am fifteen I receive his first right hook to the chin, leaving me with a visible bruise. You'd think that might be a reason to break up with your boyfriend, but no, for us it's cause to marry. We love each other in the way of crazed love, with jealousy and drama. Married as teenagers, we have two kids, and after seven years we divorce. Through it all we never question if alcohol is a problem.

Our childhoods leave us almost no other path but to find each other and battle it out. We've both grown up in worlds where parents get bloodied, strangers come and go, and along with your

ABCs you learn about the DTs, delirium tremens, the withdrawal hallucinations experienced by heavy drinkers.

It is at Sonny's that I witness a man die of alcohol poisoning. I am fourteen. I walk, as I often do, from my house on Beacon Hill down to his family's apartment near Chinatown. When I knock on the back door to the kitchen no one answers, but the door is unlocked so I enter. Sitting at the kitchen table is a man passed out, slumped over in a chair, his chin resting on his chest. The man is unimportant. I am looking for my boyfriend, and he isn't home, so I leave to check the other apartments down the alley. He's not there either. Turning back to Sonny's, I am startled to see the flashing orange-red emergency lights of an ambulance. Police stand outside the open kitchen door. I run over to find out what's happening, and learn the man at the table is dead. He has aspirated on his vomit. The orange-red lights pop on and off, illuminating the victim of drunkenness. In that pulsing light, I pay attention to him for the first time. He is American Indian, heavyset, with thick black hair just starting to grey, maybe forty or fifty years old. I wonder if he was already dead when I'd walked by earlier, but no, I don't recall seeing vomit. Does that mean he was about to choke just as I was there, and if I'd stayed I could have done something?

In retrospect, that must have been traumatic for a fourteen-year-old to witness, but at the time, I don't talk about it or ask to see a counselor or anything. I scoot past the policeman and recross the Twelfth Street Bridge back to my house, without acknowledging the whisper in my brain that tells me that man could have been my dad, could have been my mom, could have been Sonny. Could have been me.

## Lyric

Music creeps into my consciousness, a radio perhaps, or someone playing a record. Next, I feel the pain. It presses upon me from every direction. Gradually, I understand that I'm waking up.

*Where?*

I try to peek but only one eye opens, just a fraction. I close it and rest, breathing against the pain. Strands of the music become clearer. My neck throbs.

I try to roll onto my back but my body screams against movement so I stop midway.

*What happened?*

My arm aches as I raise it to wipe my eyes.

*Ouch.*

Gently, I touch the swollen eyelids. My right hand skims the surface of my face like a blind person trying to recognize someone. My bottom lip feels huge, and there's a scab on one side of it.

*Sonny.*

The night comes back to me in pieces. The party. The fight. I recall being pulled down the steps by my hair; the clunk of my head on each step. Fists. Kicks. People jostling, pulling at him, or me.

"Hey, Sonny, take it easy," they said.

He was trying to drag me to the car.

More blows.

Was I choked?

Legs towering over me, shifting legs of his friends coming to intervene.

"Hey, Sonny. Hey, man."

"Come on, buddy."

In the middle of them, I clawed at the ground until I was a few feet away and could get up and run.

That's right. I ran away.

Every set of headlights terrified me; every passing vehicle was a threat. I dove under bushes; crept behind parked cars. When I saw a city park, I dashed into its blackness. I ran from bench to tree to picnic table, making my way north.

*To my friend Bonnie's house. That's where I am.*

I recall the look on her face when she opened the door. She put me in her car and took me to the emergency room. I was assigned a battered woman's advocate.

*Under the fluorescent lights . . . on the exam table . . . then, what? We picked up the kids from the sitter. They're here. Are they here?*

I force my working eye open just enough to see through my lashes. I'm lying on Bonnie's couch. And yes, the kids are asleep on the other couch.

*Good. They're here. Oh, I hurt. And that music, why doesn't someone turn off that music?*

The tune makes its way to my brain. Tom Petty, I recognize. The lyrics come to me as if from a great distance. I concentrate, trying to make out the words.

"Somewhere . . . somehow . . . somebody must have kicked you around some . . ."

*Oh God.*

"You don't have to live like a refugee-ee. You don't . . . HAVE . . . to live like a refugee."

# Chapter 24

God chose the song I would wake to on that battered morning when I was twenty-four years old. God was there in the peach tree and in that hotel room on the day before the Oscars. God brought me Aunt Teddy. God, I finally could see, had been taking care of me my entire life.

I still wasn't sure of what it all meant to be a Christian or if I was ready to call myself one. But of the reality of God, I was certain. I continued to attend services at Bel Air Presbyterian Church, and kept up with the small group meetings in Santa Monica on Tuesday evenings. I was a baby, tasting everything for the first time with a curious hunger. Sometimes things made me laugh out loud, like being stuck in traffic and noticing the personalized license plate on the car ahead of me that read, "GD-heart symbol-U." It was as if I'd slipped into an enchanted world with messages everywhere, and it perplexed me that I had been blind to the obvious for so many years.

## Inhale

I am fifteen, standing stoned in the sunshine. There's a topless lady over there, her body shimmering and melding with all the others. Topless? I squint hard in that direction to make sure I'm not imagining it, but the lady has vanished, melting into the field of people, all in cut-offs and halter tops and . . . where's Sonny? Music pounds the air. It's the Tenino rock festival . . . we came here. I can't find him.

A flatbed truck presents itself in front of me. From up there I'll be able to see over the crowd and find the blanket where we were sitting. I'm a good climber. I climbed lots of trees when I was little. Sunlight reflects off a piece of metal on the truck, captivating me. For a second, or maybe more, I forget to climb. The laughter of two people walking by makes me turn my head at them. They're holding hands.

Sonny. Find Sonny.

I climb up on the truck and view the humanity spread out on the green, the stage in the distance, the blue sky so bright it makes me suck in my breath. Gasp. And I'm choking.

I'm choking.

I can't call out, "Hey, I'm choking," because I can't make air move, not in, not out. I spin backward and leap off the truck and there he is. A priest.

"You're choking," he says, and slaps me on the back once, twice, three times, until I cough. "Are you all right? Must have gone down the wrong tube. OK, now?"

I nod, leaning against the fender of the truck.

"You take care now, all right?"

I nod again.

He nods back at me with a grin and walks away, disappearing around the far corner of the truck. After three or four deep and beautiful breaths, I decide to follow him around the corner. But he's gone, vanished like the topless woman. But right there, not ten feet away, is the blanket with Sonny and my friends.

"Hey," I call to them. "A priest saved me."

At that, they burst out laughing. It takes a long time for them to calm down.

"No, really," I say. "He had the black shirt with the little white collar. You know? They're priests, right? With the collars? Or are they fathers or ministers, or pastors or something . . ."

"You're tripping." Sonny hands me a joint.

I had always thought it was strange that a priest was at a rock concert, but no more than that. Strange. An oddity. But looking back, as if with a new pair of eyeglasses that brought everything into focus, I marveled at how obvious God was. It's like he'd been waving a flag, saying, "I'm right here."

Even when the Man Under the House got me, God protected me. I'd never told anyone about that day, but in light of God, I saw that even that couldn't hurt me.

"Don't tell anyone," he says.

I nod.

"Don't tell anyone," he repeats.

We are in the crawl space under one of the houses in the Projects. He has a grip on my wrist.

"When you get home, your parents will ask, 'Where were you?' This is what you tell them: 'I was playing in a sandbox three blocks away.' OK?"

I nod.

"What are you going to say?"

"I was playing in a sandbox three blocks away."

At home, no one asks where I was, though my brother and sisters notice I'm covered in dirt.

"Look at Hattie. She's filthy."

"Your knees are black. So are your elbows. There's dirt in your hair."

I see their faces turned to me for an explanation.

"I was playing in a sandbox three blocks away."

No matter how much news reporters claim objectivity, there is always a bias in determining the headline, the lead to the story. In my life, the Man Under the House story was left untold, except in my psyche, perhaps, and there it was displayed under a banner headline I'd written a thousand times: *Why Did She Crawl Under the House?* The lead line might be: "While the other kids in the Projects knelt to peek at the man under the house, only Hattie responded to his beckoning and crept forward on her knees to see what he wanted."

That was the former story line. With my discovery of God's reality, the headline changed to: *Girl Isn't Killed by Man Under the House.* God was there, even there.

I've covered countless stories of children murdered by predators. I've interviewed police detectives and felt the tears of agony from grieving parents. I've walked the crime scenes, seen the shallow graves, and witnessed the faces of the guilty in court. Naturally, there were times when I considered that I too, could have been killed long ago, how "lucky" it was that I lived to tell the lie about the sandbox. It was only in that year of coming to God that I began to see that it wasn't luck. I acknowledged God's protection. He had been at my side, decade after decade. My prayers began to overflow with gratitude rather than woeful pleas for help.

"Thank you, God, for the lady who stopped me from jumping off the Twelfth Street Bridge. Thank you for Mrs. Huntington, and for the co-worker who used to wear her cross each day at CBS. Thank you for the lady in my exercise class who invited me to the Hollywood Bowl."

*There must be thousands more reasons for gratitude—millions,* I thought, ones I couldn't even guess at. I prayed thanks for every close call, every challenge, and every kindness.

"Thank you for not letting us crash and die on a 'Wake Up, We're Going to Idaho' trip. Thank you for Talmaks, and for my Indian grandparents singing Christian hymns in the Nez Perce language. Thank you for making me tough, for giving me battles so that I could handle the I Hate Hattie Club. And God, thank you for spurring me to ask 'How come?' all the time when I was small, because it trained me to become a reporter. Thank you for this career you let me have. I've gone all over the world, and I didn't even know you were the one opening the door for me."

I prayed and prayed, on my knees in the closet of the master bedroom, remembering that it was Jeanie who taught me about "prayer closets" and who first told me to read Isaiah 54.

"God, thank you for Jeanie. Thank you for help that comes from every side, all day long. Thank you for my family, for all of them, and all that we went through."

I thought of my brother John, long dead of AIDS. "He must have known you too," I whispered. With a child's "all about me" view of the world, I'd always thought Aunt Teddy was my own personal missionary. But God must have given her to all of us. John led us in prayer at meals, and each year at Christmas, he directed us in "the Program."

"Come on. It's time for the Program."

"Can I be Mary?"

"No, Lilly is Mary. I'm Joseph. The wise men are Annie, Hattie, and Carla. Lotta's the shepherd boy."

"Why am I always the shepherd boy?"

"Shhh."

"Why can't I be baby Jesus?"

"Because Baby is baby Jesus."

Mom and Dad watch the Program, sometimes sober, sometimes not. Usually they're the only people in the audience, but at least once, there are strangers there too, in various stages of inebriation, hangers-on from the bar. They talk loudly during the Program. Or fall asleep. It doesn't matter. The show goes on.

We sing Christmas carols, one after the other, ending with "Silent Night," during which Joseph, Mary, and baby Jesus take the stage, which is the hallway at the foot of our staircase, and perform the nativity of Christ.

# Chapter 25

My "thank you" prayer-a-thon had a surprising side effect: brightness. I went in to work each day with almost uncontainable joy, prompting one producer to say, "Boy, she sure got over her divorce fast." In fact, the divorce was not finished but had bogged down into a long exchange of letters from lawyer to lawyer. Despite that, I somehow beamed.

One morning, entering the building where I worked, I saw something similar in the sunny face of the security guard. She was younger than me, African American, wearing the crisp blue uniform of the security team, and entirely professional in checking my ID . . . yet, she glowed.

"Good morning," I practically sang to her.

"Good morning," she lilted back at me.

My ID back in hand, I took two or three steps away from her, heading toward the double doors that she had buzzed to unlock for me, but at the last second I swiveled around to examine her cheery face once more. Spontaneously I sang out, "This little light of mine . . ."

Without missing a beat, she sang back, "I'm going to let it shine . . ."

Together we finished, "Let it shine, let it shine, let it shine."

I waved at her, then passed through the door and walked down the carpeted hall to my office, aware that being with God meant turning the world upside down. Television City, like most studios in Los Angeles, is a status-conscious place. The very door I had entered was labeled "The Artists' Entrance" as if only those whose faces appeared on television could walk through it: the actors in the soaps, the celebrities who drop by the talk shows, the occasional news anchor. Next in the strata would be the executives and producers who craft the shows into being. At the bottom were those who kept the buildings operational such as the mail room clerks, maintenance crews, and security guards. Yet the guard and I were sisters singing in the same choir, shining our light.

It wasn't as if I had been brought "down" to the level of a security guard or she had been brought "up" to the level of an on-air person. It was that those levels were themselves meaningless, which in a rush I realized was an absolute relief to me. I had always felt uncomfortable with the status afforded a news correspondent, perhaps because the poverty of my childhood had left me feeling chronically inferior.

## Balancing

I am in junior high school, in the eighth grade, when a teacher tells me to go to the office. Someone wants to see me, I'm told. I don't know who, or why.

At the principal's office I'm directed into the counselor's room, but the person waiting there is not the school counselor. She is one of the ladies from the American Indian Women's Service League. She tells me that I am smart, and she wants to help me in life. She places before me a multiple-choice quiz and asks me to take the test right now, right here, this minute. Fill it all out, she says, because there is a private school "back east" that wants to give a scholarship to an Indian child. "Back east" to me means the reservation in Idaho, or maybe Spokane.

"You're smart," the woman says. "You could get this scholarship."

A few months later, I'm at the airport hugging everyone good-bye like the time I went to Mexico, only this time my ticket reads "New York."

"Thought I'd be the first to New York," says John, who is in college studying to be an actor.

"Bye, you guys."

"Write to us."

"I will, and if Aunt Teddy calls, tell her where I am, OK?"

"We will."

"And don't forget to write back to me."

"We will."

"Bye, bye, everyone."

The scholarship allows me to live and learn with the elite from New York and Boston and places I don't even know about. The day after I arrive at Kent School for Girls in Connecticut, there is a Tea at the headmaster's house to welcome new students. The scene is nothing like the time I shared tea with Rena in her tiny apartment at the Pike Place Market. At the headmaster's Tea, the girls are in dresses and the few male teachers are in jackets and ties. People chat in twos or threes, mostly standing, though a few are perched on floral patterned chairs set here and there. Balancing my teacup on its saucer, I survey these new surroundings, uncertain where to place myself. Flowers, fruit, and trays of sandwiches are piled so artfully on a table draped in white that it strikes me the long table could be a stage and the food the star. *We should all clap*, I think, inwardly applauding the display. Beyond the table, white-trimmed doors open to a stone porch and a backyard of astonishing green where I spot more people walking or standing with the same little cups in their hands. Bits of laughter float by.

"Hi," says a voice.

I turn to take in the interested eyes of a tall woman wearing glasses.

"I'm Miss Gassett. I'm a counselor here." She saves me from being alone at the tea and at the school.

In the next weeks and months, I grasp the routine of a prep school: a roommate, a uniform, an expectation that every student excel. With the help of a tutor secured by Miss Gassett, I catch up in algebra, break through in Latin, do well in English, and become one of the girls—almost.

There are stables on campus where some students keep their horses. Wearing dark round helmets, odd-looking pants, and high boots, they ride their sleek mounts round and round the corral, while an instructor shouts out things like "change your lead," whatever that means. I watch, hoping they'll bring out the jumps for the horses to leap over. Now and then, I daydream about "un caballo que corre's" gallop into the desert.

On Wednesdays and Sundays we have chapel. I'd never heard of an Episcopalian service but that's what it's called. The services are in an old stone church, with dark wood benches and candlelight. I participate the same way I do with the horses . . . watching, in the setting but not a part of it.

Who knows, maybe in time I would have become one with them, but instead, one night I hear something that ends it all for me.

It happens at the start of evening study hall, when we're supposed to turn off the music of our stereos and spend the next two hours at work in our dorm rooms. Just as I reach for the knob to turn off the small radio on my desk, I hear the unmistakable beat of a drum, an Indian powwow drum.

Intrigued, I duck my head lower into the cubicle, leaning closer to the tiny speaker, seeking more of the drumming, and find that it was part of a brief news report about Indians taking over Alcatraz Island, demanding the tribes get a piece of America back. When the announcer goes on to the next story, the budget problems of Mayor Lindsey, I turn the radio off.

Indians fighting back? I wish I could replay the report. It was too brief. I want more. Switching the radio back on only brings more about the budget of New York, which annoys me. I'm suddenly angry. I want to hear about Indians drumming and taking America back, not about budgets and money. The wealthy girls at this school have no concept of budgets. They never worry about money. One is the daughter of a Central American dictator, others hope to date the Kennedy son who attends the nearby boys' prep.

In a swirl of resentment, I picture home in Seattle, where there's no concept of a budget either because there's no money to manage. Recalling Baby's one-year birthday and the time we split a cupcake six ways, I get furious.

"We ate what we could find," I want to yell. But there's no one to yell at. My roommate is in the library and I am sitting here, hating all of the rich girls in all of the rooms just like this one. *They don't deserve all they have*, I think. They turned up their noses at the Lobster Newburg in the dining hall. They complain about eggs at breakfast and grumble that Salisbury steak isn't really steak.

I want a warpath.

The next morning at breakfast, I slip a knife off the table and hide it in my book bag. Back in my dorm room I stash it in my drawer. My thievery has begun. Over the next weeks, I add spoons, forks, even a serving utensil. Eventually, I pack up my haul into a shoebox, wrap it with brown paper, and write my parents' address on it.

I imagine them opening it. A present from Hattie, they'll say. Look what she sent us! But then I worry that Dad will hock the silverware, remembering that Mom was always blowing up at him for his trips to the pawnshop.

"Where's the clock radio?" she'd demand. He'd ignore her. Later, it might be the record player that would vanish.

It doesn't occur to me that silverware isn't food. I don't take the time to ask myself if USDA surplus commodity powdered eggs would taste any better on a fancy fork. None of it matters anyway. My plan to send a present home fails.

Miss Gassett, who's been so kind to me since the day I arrived scared and poorly dressed, calls me into her office. When she puts the package on her desk, I know it's over.

"What were you thinking?" she asks.

I don't have an answer. Indian drums and Alcatraz bang about my brain but can't jell into a logical explanation.

She assures me that I can keep my scholarship. They are not throwing me out. That's when my mouth forms words to throw myself out.

"I want to go home."

"Hattie, we're not sending you home. We want to help you. Tell me, why did you do this?"

"I want to go home." I bound to my feet in their nice new shoes, the ones the school gave me to match my uniform, the best shoes I've ever owned. Without the slightest understanding of what I was doing, I create my exit.

Within a week, I am back in the "haunted" house at the top of the concrete staircase, where the cuckoo clock goes off at random times and where electronic items vanish overnight.

"Where's the electric coffeemaker?" Mom yells. "Did your dad take the coffeemaker?"

I never really tell them why I am home. They never really ask.

## Was It You, God?

And we know that in all things God works for the good of those who love him, who have been called according to his purpose. (Rom. 8:28)

I was working my way through the New Testament and gradually getting a new perspective not only on the present drudgery of the divorce but also on my past. The prep school incident had been an embarrassing regret that I'd carried with me for much of my life. Now, I saw that even though I had thrown away God's gift of the scholarship, he hadn't given up on me—certainly not on my soul and not on my life path, either.

A couple of years after walking away from the prep school, I was in high school in Seattle, and I proclaimed one day, "Who needs white man's education. I'm going to quit school." It was then that a community leader named Bernie White Bear happened to be calling on the Kauffman family. Just as I was making my proclamation, hopping down the concrete steps two at a time, Bernie halted me in my tracks by saying, "Hattie, we don't need more Indian *dropouts*. We need more Indian *graduates*."

Certain now that God had put Bernie there, I scanned back over the years, looking for more of God's nudges. *Was it you, God, who sent that awkward guy to our Indian student meeting in college, the guy who had the unlikely idea of a daily five-minute broadcast called "Indian News"?*

Later, I was offered a broadcast journalism scholarship because an executive from WCCO television in Minneapolis happened to hear me on the radio. *Was it you, God, who caused the man to turn on his car radio at the exact moment that I was giving my report on Indian News?*

In hindsight, one can always see what one wants to see: inclination coloring interpretation. Reason finds a way to argue.

Sonny died of diabetes long after we had divorced and gone our separate ways. Why didn't God save him? Or what about my good and talented brother, John? Why did he have to die before AZT and the AIDS cocktail were discovered?

There was much I didn't understand, but as spring turned to summer in 2007, there was one thing I was certain of: God.

# Chapter 26

"A blind date?"

"Yes," said my co-worker. "I wasn't sure if you'd be interested, since . . . well, he's an oncologist. Is that awkward, you know, since you had cancer?"

"A date?" I repeated.

"He has tickets to the Sting concert and is looking for someone to go with him. I told him I knew a newly divorced woman."

*I'm not actually divorced yet. But wow—a date.*

"Are you interested?" she asked.

"Uh, yeah, I guess."

"It doesn't bother you that he's an oncologist?" she asked again.

"It's not like he's going to examine me."

Of all nights—the concert fell on the evening before our first big court hearing. Could this be the best distraction for what the next morning would hold, or would I be a wreck the whole night? The prospect of being face-to-face with my husband in divorce court made me want to jump out of my skin. I was petitioning the court to have him removed from the house and I knew he'd be enraged. Why I cared about him being angry was a mystery—but I did. Still.

Our case was the first thing on the docket the next morning at a downtown courthouse. I booked a hotel room near the courthouse, thinking it would save me a rush-hour trip across town. Besides, I reasoned, it put me right next to the Staples Center, where my big date was happening.

Walking from my room to the concert, my anxiety was so high I wanted to shout to passersby, "I'm going to divorce court tomorrow. Comfort me. Will someone give me a hug? I'm going to divorce court tomorrow!"

*But right now, I'm going on a blind date.*

I looked down at my feet prancing forward—even they seemed to betray my awkward nervousness. I could only laugh at my life.

*I'm going to divorce court. No, I'm going on a date.*

*I'm going to see my husband. No, I'm going to meet a stranger.*

*The ants go marching two by two, hoorah, hoorah.*

The music in the concert was deafening, and the lighting minimal. I used the occasional flashes of light from the stage to sneak better looks at my date: fifties, maybe sixty, another aging Boomer, grayish hair, glasses, crisp striped shirt, jeans. The noise made it nearly impossible for getting-to-know-you questions.

"Where do you live?"

"Brentwood."

"Where?"

"Brentwood."

"Westwood?"

"BRENTWOOD."

Since we couldn't share information, we began to shout comments about the music whenever the din allowed.

Sting sang, "I'll be watching you . . ."

"THE STALKER'S ANTHEM," I yelled.

My date smiled. I'm pretty sure he had no idea what I'd said. I began to relax.

*OK, this isn't so difficult. Maybe court won't be either.*

When we finally spilled out with the crowd onto the summer sidewalk, he asked me if I wanted a ride back to Brentwood.

"Oh no, I have a hotel room here," I answered.

"Well," he smiled, "I'll accompany you, then." I thought it was gentlemanly of him to walk me back to my hotel. He picked up the pace.

"Drink?" he asked, once we were in the lobby.

"No thanks, I don't drink."

"So have a ginger ale." He grabbed my hand and turned into the bar.

*Weird, we're holding hands.*

I had to tell myself that not everyone in the bar was thinking, *Oh look, they're holding hands.* Still, I wiggled free. Once seated, with drinks in front of us, I explained that I was going to divorce court in the morning and was quite anxious.

"Oh, don't worry," he said. "Nothing happens in divorce court. I've been stuck in it for years."

"Years?"

"Yes, trust me. Nothing will happen tomorrow. Your lawyer will stand up and say something. His lawyer will stand up and say something. The judge will say something, then everybody leaves and you do it again in six months."

*Years?*

Disheartened, I slumped into the dark leather couch.

"Oh, chin up," he said, signaling for another Scotch while slipping his arm around me. When he pulled me into him, I was momentarily more shocked at the softness of his body than at his presumption.

*How "fleshy" he feels. How odd to be held by a stranger. How long has it been since a man embraced me?*

I was distracted by my thoughts, until his hands began to caress me.

"Um," I objected, pulling back.

"Oh, relax," he urged, reaching for me again. "We deserve this."

"No! I . . . I've to got to get to bed . . . Court is at eight . . ."

"OK." He smiled. "That's fine." He quickly downed his drink, paid the check, and turned to me, happily. As we walked out of the bar, he put his arm around my waist.

"Which way to the elevator?" he sang to the hostess.

*He thinks he's coming to my hotel room.*

He squeezed me tighter.

*There's the elevator.*

He pushed the "up" button.

I jumped away from him.

"Really great to meet you," I exclaimed, sticking out my hand for a shake.

His eyebrows rose as his jaw dropped. Simultaneously, the elevator opened and I hopped inside, pushing any button just to get the thing operating. His mouth was still agape as the doors began to close.

"I want to see you again," he belted. As the doors shut, I heard him shout: "Soon!"

I fell back against the wall.

*I'm not ready to date.*

Morning came quickly, and with it, heavy dread. The time had come to confront the man I'd spent half a year evading, and despite my newfound certainty in God, I resisted. Getting dressed took effort. Bending to put on my shoes was arduous. It felt like I wouldn't get out the door unless someone carried me. I dragged myself to the bedside table, in search of a Gideon's Bible. With lifeless hands I lifted it, and turned to Psalms.

> He is my defense;
> I shall not be moved. (Ps. 62:6 NKJV)

*God is my defense.*

Each step down the hallway echoed the refrain. Out of the hotel, and onto the street, I repeated, "God is my defense."

I was still repeating it, "God is my defense. He is my defense.

You are my defense," as I entered the courthouse and found my way to the correct floor. My stomach was a knot of nerves. I'd been inside plenty of courthouses during my decades as a news reporter, but it was a different and unwelcome feeling knowing that this was *my* case rather than one I was assigned to cover. My attorneys waved for me to join them where they were sitting, on a bench midway down the cold hallway. I maneuvered my way to sit between them so that they might flank me.

Out of the corner of my eye, I recognized the long, loping gait of the man I had once married—arriving for this, my petition that he be removed from our home.

When our case was called and we moved inside, things began to blur for me. First one lawyer then another stood, talked, sat, stood again, their chairs making an irritating scooting sound each time they moved to and fro. My mind meandered, recalling what my date from the night before had said, that nothing ever happens in court. I hoped that wouldn't prove true. Just then, the quiet in the room caught my attention. The papers had all been presented back and forth, and now everyone was looking at the judge. For several minutes he said nothing, his silence engulfing us. I wondered how many other sad and broken lives had paraded before him.

"This is thin," commented the judge at last.

My lawyers had warned me that we had only a slim chance of getting the order. I turned my head to the left, where a high window revealed a narrow strip of white-grey Los Angeles sky.

*God, you are my defense. I turn my life and my will over to you.*

"But there's something here," the judge went on.

The sound of his gavel made us all jump.

"I'm going to grant it. Respondent has twenty-four hours to vacate the property."

It didn't make the divorce final, but the resounding bang of the gavel ended the absurdity of cohabitation. I nearly wept with relief. After eight months of living like a refugee, I was one step closer to . . . what? I didn't know what might follow the end of my second marriage. But experience had shown me that life—no, that God—would make a road for me.

## TV Reporter

After Sonny, I end up back in Seattle. I am twenty-five, the mom of a five-year-old boy and three-year-old girl, and jobless. I move into the attic of my aging and no longer raucous parents and begin applying for jobs. It being Seattle, I think I might find something at Boeing. But within months comes the chance to be a TV reporter.

My first day in the newsroom of the NBC affiliate, the managing editor hands me off to the show producer.

"This is our minority reporter apprentice," she says. "Can she trail you so she can learn how a newscast comes together?"

He nods, and passes me off to his production assistant, a chubby young woman who always seems out of breath.

"Follow me," she orders, darting out of the room with a stack of papers in her hands.

"These are the scripts," she says over her shoulder, ". . . one copy to each anchor, another to the control room, another set for the teleprompter."

She climbs a flight of steps, puffing as she speeds along. I clip-clop behind her. At the top of the stairs she turns and frowns at my feet. I am dressed as I think a news reporter should be, in a suit, nylon stockings, and pumps.

"That'll never do," she says, and sticks her foot out for me to see. "You need some of these. You're going to be running all over this place. Sneakers are the only way to go."

She dashes ahead.

*Wrong,* I think. *I'm not here to train for your job. I'm here to become a reporter.*

The next day I wear higher heels.

When I get my chance to actually report a TV news story, I am almost immobilized by the fear that I might make a mistake.

*What if I get a fact wrong? What if I go on the air with something that isn't perfect?*

Each day I go to work with a churning in my gut. In the news business, there's always something to make a stomach clench: deadlines; live shots; the pressure to look good, sound good, and get the facts right. I walk around with the same ever-present inner tension that I experienced as a child. *Everything is OK*, I tell myself, just as I had at age four or five, knowing that at any second chaos could crumble it all.

I don't know if I can really do the job of news reporter, but I *have* to do it because there are bills to pay and I have two small children. I've moved out of my parents' place, scraped together a down payment on a house, and feel the weight of a mortgage and the knowledge that no one else but me is responsible for keeping it all afloat.

Many of the others in the newsroom are in their twenties like I am, but unlike me, they are single, childless, and carefree. There are also other reminders that we are different.

One night, a cameraman and I are sitting in a news car on a stakeout, waiting for someone to exit a building downtown so we can run up and try to get an interview. As the minutes turn to hours, I get restless. Tapping fingers on the dash, gazing out the window at people walking past on the crowded sidewalks, shifting in my seat—it all starts to feel familiar.

"Hey," I say. "This reminds me of sitting in the car when I was a kid waiting for my parents to come out of a bar." Not looking at him, I crane my head around to see if the old tavern might still be there.

"It was right around here," I continue, trying to look out the back window. "Seven of us kids, stuck in a car waiting . . ."

That's when I turn around and see his expression. He is aghast.

Oh. Maybe I should keep quiet.

In time, I do make my way at that TV station. It's basic math. Subtract the commercials, the weather and sports reports, and there are only about sixteen or seventeen minutes of news time during each half-hour newscast. With more reporters than minutes to fill, the ones who get on the air are the ones willing to cover any story, anywhere, at any time.

I begin volunteering to work holidays, night shifts, anything to increase my odds. One reporter teases, "Hattie Kauffman, you'd cover the rats having a meeting in the sewer at midnight." And it's true; I never say no. Work becomes my engine, powering my days and eventually, my years.

Later, when I become the first Native American news correspondent for a national broadcast, it is only because that attitude has been drilled into me. I don't work for *World News Tonight* with Peter Jennings—I just happen to be in Hawaii when a United Airlines jet takes off from the islands and begins to tear apart. The fuselage peels back like a banana skin as the jet returns for an emergency landing. I don't even know it has happened. I am asleep in my hotel room when the phone rings.

"It's ABC News in New York. Hattie Kauffman?"

The voice on the line asks if I can cover the story for that day's broadcast.

"Of course," I say. "I'll do it."

Because of the time difference between Hawaii and New York, I have only a few hours to race to the airport, interview passengers, shoot my on-camera stand up, write the story, and work with the producer and editor to get it cut and fed back to New York. It is a frenzied few hours made intense by the time pressure, but otherwise I am just a reporter doing what a reporter does. It isn't until years later that I learn that that story, in 1989, marks the first time a Native American has ever filed a report on a network evening news broadcast.

It's just Hattie, from the Projects.

A decade later, when someone at work tells me I have a message from the White House, I think they're kidding. By now I am working for CBS News in Los Angeles. I am not in the DC Bureau. I am not working on any story that would involve the White House. Refusing to fall for some producer's practical joke, I ignore the message. An hour later the receptionist's voice comes over the intercom: "Hattie, pick up line A. You have a call from the White House." OK, I pick up.

It is the First Lady's office. And it's not a joke, but an invitation. First Lady Hillary Clinton will be unveiling the new Sacagawea coin, I am told, and in her speech she wishes to acknowledge Native American women who are path makers, forging new ground as the young Shoshone woman did for the explorers Lewis and Clark. My presence is requested because the First Lady would like to refer to me. Incredulous, I take the receiver from my ear for one beat to stare at it. Mrs. Huntington had once scrubbed dirt off my face and now I am taking a call from the White House of the United States of America, telling me that I am a "path maker" like Sacagawea.

As I looked back on the start of my TV career, I saw that I was the one who had been guided, constantly presented with a path while simultaneously being pursued. Only God can do both at once.

## Home

I bought a dozen white roses for myself.

As I pulled into the garage for the first time, I began to sing, "I'm home, and it's my house." Stepping onto the limestone of the entryway, my song evolved into a wailing chant: "I'm hooooooooooooooooome. And its myyyyyyyyyyyy house."

I stretched my arms overhead, and turned slowly, taking in the rooms.

*I'm home. And it's my house.*

I twirled, danced, and sang my song.

"The kitchen, this is my kitchen," I said aloud. Opening the fridge, I saw that he'd cleared out all the food.

*I don't care. I can buy what I want to eat.*

I sat on the couch, free to be in the spacious living room. My eye took in the dining table, where I would get to eat.

To my right was the big-screen TV, from which he had once banned the show that employed me. I located the remote so that I could put the channel back to the network that carried my show.

*That's strange. No power.*

Realizing he must have disconnected the service, I smiled at the big black screen.

*Not to worry. I'll get you fixed up and back in the swing of things in no time.*

In truth, it took longer than I expected to regain a sense of normalcy at home. At night, I retreated to my bedroom and bolted the lock as if there were an intruder in the house. Over the next few days, I emerged slowly, taking stock in brief forays about the place, which still had an alien feel to it. The multiple signed rock guitars were gone, but the big bolts and screws that had held them up remained, sticking out of the living room and entryway walls like scars. Getting someone to patch and paint was more than I could contend with at that point, so I looked the other way and focused on doing the little things. I had a locksmith rekey everything and changed the code for the alarm system. That helped me sleep better. So did the Bible, which I read every night.

The LORD will fight for you; you need only to be still. (Exod. 14:14)

I began to cook and to sit down at the table to eat. At Whole Foods, I bought the kind of groceries *I* wanted. It was such a joy I almost pranced down the aisles. I baked again, and yearned to invite people to my house to join me for a meal. But the interior wasn't quite ready for that.

In time, many of the personal items that I had squished into the master bedroom began to make their way back to the living and dining rooms: prized books, photos of Phoenix, Native American art. I put those unsightly bolts in the walls to use, hanging Indian beadwork from them. My grandmother's beaded bags with floral designs I hung in the living room. In the entryway, I used the old guitar bolts to hang a breastplate, the kind a warrior might have worn, made of narrow bones strung on buckskin with feathers adorning the sides. I was reinhabiting my home.

Finally, I burned sage in the doorways, the old Indian ritual of protection.

*Do Christians get to do Indian rituals? I'm such a baby in my faith, I don't know anything. But this feels right. Pray for protection, in the name of Jesus, while burning sage.*

# Chapter 27

"Come on, we can do it," Carla urges, nodding, her suntanned face inches from my own.

Squatting by the fence post, we peer at the horse.

"We don't even have a rope," I say, and immediately regret my protest. I'm the older sister. I shouldn't be the one to make excuses. But that's the way it is with Carla. Her spunk often leads me, like the time she had me trying not to laugh when Mom threw the bowl of canned peas at Dad, or the time we turned the tables on the mean dogs in our neighborhood. Carla and I were about seven and nine years old then, I think. It was a windy day, the kind with puffy white clouds racing by, when we felt so powerful we declared it "Dog Chasing Day," and jumped off our porch to go chase dogs, fearless.

"A rope . . ." Carla mutters, bringing me back to the present moment. She looks around at the dry field, unknown territory to us, and steps away from me, her feet crunching on the brittle grass. We are on the Oregon reservation of Lilly's new husband, a hot plateau, rocky and dry, here to babysit Lilly's new son. But this is not a babysitting day, this is a horse wrangling day.

"How's this?" she says, returning with a bit of bailing twine.

The twine is less than a yard long, a pitiful piece of orange string, frayed at both ends.

"It'll do." I nod, determined not to back out even though a thin length of twine is not a rope, not a bridle, and certainly not a saddle.

Stepping on the lower rung of barbed wire, I lift the wire above it so that Carla can crouch between the two and pass through. Once inside the pasture, she does the same for me and we begin our coaxing of the horse. Carla makes kissing sounds as we creep cautiously toward it. I hold my arm straight out in front of me, with my palm extended flat the way it would be if I were holding an apple for the horse—which I'm not, because we don't have an apple, a carrot, a sugar cube, or any of the things you're supposed to have to lure a horse.

The animal lifts its head to study us, flicking its ears. It is light brown with a darker mane and tail. When the horse shifts a hoof, raising it slightly, we stop in our tracks. After a second, Carla coos some indecipherable sound, and leans forward again. Together, we continue our approach on this, the third horse we have tried to catch today.

Unlike the others, it doesn't bolt. To our utter amazement, it remains fixed in place. In moments, we are beside it, fumbling about with this unexpected opportunity to actually do what we set out to do.

"OK, put the rope around his neck."

"OK, got it."

"Easy, easy there."

We pat and touch the horse, reassuring it. *Easy. Easy.* And now what do we do? Carla on one side of the horse's neck, me on the other, patting, murmuring, twitching about in our nervousness, uncertain how to proceed.

"I'll boost you, OK?"

"OK."

We keep saying OK. We keep saying *easy*. And Carla's bending low and I'm stepping into her clasped palms and I'm facedown on the hot hairs of the horse's back. *Easy. Easy. OK.* Swing up.

Where's the twine? Grab the mane . . . what a coarse, thick nest of hair. And it's slipping through my hands. No, that's me slipping. What happened to the twine? There's the sky. And I'm down in a thud on the tinder-dry earth, looking up at Carla, who is laughing, tears in her eyes, bent at the waist. I turn my head toward the horse, expecting it has galloped off in a cloud of dust, but it's only a few feet away, back to chewing grass, ignoring us. Elbows on the ground, I tilt my head up at the heavens and laugh aloud with my little sister, loving her and this day.

She rides next.

Then it's my turn again.

And hers.

## But, Jesus?

Heaven. That's what I thought the "kingdom of God" was. But the expression on the faces in the room looked dubious when I said it. The Tuesday-night small group in Santa Monica was wrestling with the parable of the mustard seed.

"Let's read that section again," suggested the leader. "'Finally, Jesus said: What is God's kingdom like? What story can I use to explain it? It is like what happens when a mustard seed is planted in the ground. It is the smallest seed in all the world. But once it is planted, it grows larger than any garden plant. It even puts out branches that are big enough for birds to nest in its shade'" (Mark 4:30–32 CEV).

"The kingdom goes on into heaven," suggested a young woman who always rode her bike to the meeting, giving me a look that said, *you were partially right*. "But it starts here on earth where the seed is sown."

"We are the kingdom," sighed the screenwriter, leaning back into the couch.

"We?" I asked.

In the room sat a cop, a schoolteacher, an unemployed actor, a lawyer, a nurse, an accountant, a writer, a doctor, the cyclist, and me, a news correspondent. *We are the kingdom of God?*

"Well, look back a few paragraphs, in the same chapter. Jesus is telling the apostles that they get the secret of the kingdom. That would mean, yeah, right now in this lifetime . . ."

While the leader of the group scanned the text, the rest of us dropped our eyes to the Bibles on our laps.

"Mine is a different translation," one said. "But you're right. At Mark 4:11, Jesus says, 'The secret of the kingdom of God has been given to you.'"

"Wait. You're saying that because Jesus was telling the apostles that they get to know the kingdom . . . and because we, in this room, are today's version of students of Jesus . . . that that means everything he says to them, he is saying to us?"

Nods met my question, a circle of warm, friendly faces. No one said, "Well, duh!" But I felt myself getting a hint, a flicker of light.

Jesus. I hadn't wanted to think much about Jesus. It had felt revolutionary enough for me to admit aloud the touch upon my head. It was already a new world for me, with God and Bible verses that seemed to speak to me. *But Jesus? Hey, if you've got Bible verses speaking directly to you, why not this verse? To you it is given to know the mystery. Why would you stop there?*

To me, it is given to know the mystery.

I wanted to announce, "Hey, I'm getting it," but seeing that the study had moved on, I returned to my own whirling thoughts. Their conversation became a background murmur with isolated sentences emerging as if to punctuate my new insights.

"This whole section is Jesus teaching on the kingdom of God."

"Right here it says it's like a seed that grows of itself."

"It's actually Jesus doing the sowing."

# Chapter 28

The clang of the bell woke me, muffled as it was by tall Ponderosa pines. It was dawn at Talmaks. I'd never imagined returning here as an adult. From what I'd heard, the summer retreats hosted by the Presbyterians had nearly died out. But something pulled me back as I waited for resolution in the divorce, so I called my sister Jo Ann, who had a cabin there, and made arrangements for my grandson and me to spend time at the camp.

And now the bell was calling. I quickly slipped on jeans and a sweater, trying not to awaken Jo Ann in the next bunk. Tiptoeing across the wooden floor, I emerged into the cool, fragrant air. The pine carpet was soft underfoot as I walked over to the tipi. The bell clanged again as I lifted the tipi flap to check on Phoenix. He was curled up in his sleeping bag, exhausted from playing with his cousins around last night's campfire.

Less than a dozen of us gathered in the church "tent" at the center of the campground for the sunrise service. When I was a child, it really was a big canvas tent held up by what seemed to be giant log timbers that took the men of the tribe days to erect and take down each summer. These days, there was more efficiency but less beauty in the "tent"; a corrugated tin roof stood over a cement pad, set in the center of the open field. Around the central grassy area were the family camps; tipis, small sleep cabins, old outhouses, modern port-a-potties were all dispersed among the Ponderosa that had watched over Talmaks for more than a century. The camp had been created by six Nez Perce Presbyterian churches on the reservation following a contentious split in the late 1800s between the Christian Indians and those who had rejected the white man's religion.

"Do we have any prayer requests?" that morning's leader asked. There followed the typical requests for the aging and ailing. I loved prayer time. Each day my prayer was for protection and God's guidance. We broke into small groups of three or four and huddled together, our hands on each other's shoulders, our hearts united in desiring the best for one another. Fortified, we wandered back to our separate camps to prepare breakfast for sleepy kids.

I'd brought Phoenix here to share with him some of the joy that I remembered from childhood: hot dogs around the fire, foot races, camp picnics, and happy shrieks on the hot afternoons as we plunged our bodies into the cold Salmon River.

The wind in the pines was the sound of peace to me, as reassuring as the weathered but surviving cook cabin my grandfather had built. Jo Ann's initials, carved into the doorframe almost fifty years ago, were still visible. Down at the spring, my sister Lilly's initials were carved into a crumbling piece of wood. L. K. plus . . . her old boyfriend's initials had faded.

Talmaks was an escape for us as kids. But it wasn't until now that I appreciated its true purpose. It was a Christian retreat for members of our tribe. When I was little, the clanging bell didn't mean much. But now it was balm to me, as it must have been to my grandparents.

*The trees look just the same as they did back then.*

I swung back and forth in Jo Ann's hammock, looking up at the tops of the towering Ponderosa. Their long needles were black against the vibrant blue of the sky.

"You mean people have been coming here their whole lives?" Phoenix demanded in outrage when he realized he hadn't been introduced to Talmaks until age seven. "Grammie, how come we don't have our own cabin?"

"Well," I answered, "maybe we can build one."

He skipped off, excited.

*Shall I build a sleep cabin, claim my ground, commit to this Christian camp? Christianity is nothing less than a commitment. You can't be half born again.*

I thought about Jeanie. And, I considered my artist friend with all her crystals, Shiva statues, I-ching, Buddha, Yoga invocations, and silent Dharma retreats.

*Is faith really a smorgasbord? I'll have a little of the applesauce because it soothes me now? When that stops working, I'll nibble on something else?*

I thought about my favorite producer, an orthodox Jew who in her entire life had never wandered from one faith to another.

Everyone is trying to believe something, even the atheist.

There was no denying the Bible's effect upon me. From the moment I'd read "Let God be your husband" my life had changed—or was it just my view of life? No, my life truly was different, and had been clearly so since the day in February when I'd felt the touch on my head.

And once you know that, you can't go back to unknowing.

*But Hattie, are you ready to announce: "I believe in Jesus"?*

I kept getting hung up on the fact that I was a news correspondent. *I'm not supposed to "believe," I'm supposed to report the facts. On top of that, I'm an American Indian.*

## Buckskin Strips

I am fifteen. My long hair is braided as if it's the 1800s, tied with buckskin strips. I wear a fringed leather jacket, blue jeans, and attitude.

"Christianity destroyed the Indians," I spit into the phone, breaking Aunt Teddy's heart. "It was just another way to take our land."

"Hattie," she begins.

It's been three years since Teddy and I said good-bye at the airport in Oklahoma City: thirty-six months of scraping my hide tough. With more defiance than I can shoulder, I turn on an easy target, uncoiling contempt at white people and their God. I hate that Indians lost all the battles, hate that I grew up poor, hate that there is no one or nothing that can be counted on.

"I don't want any more Christian talk. I don't want to hear it anymore. I'm finished with it."

Without saying good-bye, I hand the receiver away, unaware that I will never get another opportunity to talk to Teddy.

## Past the Point

"Grammie," Phoenix called, shaking away my memories. "Pitch the pinecone to me." He had a light plastic bat in hand. The ball that had come with it was long ago lost in the brush.

"OK, I'm coming." I rolled off the hammock at Talmaks, wondering which faith Phoenix would choose. It had already dawned on him that this Indian gathering wasn't like the powwows he'd attended on previous trips to the reservation. As we sat on the wooden pews during a service one morning, he'd whispered loudly, "Grammie, I don't get it. What does Jesus have to do with Indians?"

"Tell you later," I had said, but then hadn't gotten around to it. I realized now that I would have to. I felt the responsibility inside to tell Phoenix, to tell everyone . . .

"Come on, pitch a pinecone right here." He swung the bat in the strike zone.

I smiled at him, knowing my faith was past the point of no return.

*I am a Christian.*

# Chapter 29

Carla and I are playing with dolls. Each doll has only one leg, but we disguise that by putting one of Dad's socks on each doll and pulling it all the way up over her chest so that the sock looks like a long, strapless evening gown. One wears a white sock gown, and the other a black sock gown. We're pleased with our gowns and happily playing, until we hear Lilly say, "Shadow's gone."

"Gone?"

We drop our dolls in their fancy dresses.

"What happened? Where is he?"

"He's gone," John says, walking in from the back door.

"Did he break his chain again?" Annie calls, as she comes running down the stairs, two at a time.

"No," Lilly jumps in. "He's really . . . gone."

"How come?"

Carla and I get up to follow the older ones to the back door where Shadow is supposed to be. His chain lies on the hard packed dirt. Little piles of poop are all that's left of him.

"Dad gave him away. He was too wild . . ." John lets his voice drift away.

"Gave him away?" Annie asks.

"Yep, 'cause he escaped too many times, and he bit that one lady."

"He gave Shadow away?"

"To a junkyard. Dad said they want mean dogs to guard the junkyards."

"But . . . but . . . he's not mean."

"People don't know that. If they think he's mean, they'll stay away."

Annie starts to cry and stomps past us to go back upstairs, where she slams a door.

The rest of us remain staring at the space where Shadow used to be.

"But," I ask, "who's going to bark and keep us safe from bad guys? Who's going to guard us?"

## Jesus Watched

I discovered the Jesus of the Garbage Dump months ago, when I used to drive aimlessly in the early morning hours while waiting for my husband to leave the house. One morning, I got the idea to drive up the backside of a hill that towered over our street. From a public parking lot at the top, I thought, I might be able to spy on our house below and watch him pull his car out of the garage, and thereby know if I could return home.

But the first time I went up there and peered over the cliff, the rooftops in view were of homes about a block from mine. In order to see our house I needed a vantage point farther up the hill, past the edge of the parking lot, which meant entering the private property of a Catholic college that sat at the crest. At the entrance stood a statue of the Virgin Mary and behind that, a guard shack.

*What do I say to the guard? "Don't mind me, I'm just spying on my own house"?*

I was too embarrassed for that, so to avoid the guard, I journeyed on foot through the wet weeds along the ridgeline. That's how I happened upon Jesus of the Garbage Dump.

Walking on what seemed to be a deer trail, I began to notice the distinct smell of spoiled food. As I broke through the woody brush, the source of the smell came into view: two dumpsters filled with refuse from the campus. The unpleasantness almost made me turn back, but I wondered if I might be able to see my house from the edge of the clearing. I continued forward, and there he was, Jesus on a cross: a fifteen-foot statue set at the edge of the clearing, looking down on the dumpsters.

*Why here? Shouldn't he be in the center of the campus?*

I passed by Jesus and found a spot where I could peer down the hill at my house. It was a routine I would repeat countless times, and in the early days I merely scurried past the Jesus statue on my way to the outlook and again as I rushed back to my car after determining the coast was clear for me to go into my own house. But all of that was before the touch on my head, before I joined a church and started praying with my small group each week. It was before I'd given him my heart, my life.

On this day, I hiked up the hill to revisit the place, my first return since my life had been transformed. Crossing through the weeds, I again smelled the refuse from the dumpsters. At the clearing, this utter neglect of the Lord's image cut me to the quick. Scraps of trash littered the ground—plastic, paper, small pieces of metal or glass. Bugs swam on a stagnant dark puddle at the foot of the cross. It appeared that the place had once been loved; remnants of a picket fence leaned against each other, the metal peeling and bent. It must have surrounded a fountain and flower beds.

"Lord . . ."

I felt somewhat odd, praying at the garbage dump, but I closed my eyes knowing that the Greatness I addressed was not confined to the place.

"God, thank you for taking care of me, for protecting me and getting me through all that I went through this year . . ."

As I mumbled on, the prayers of gratitude evolved on their own, into apologies.

"Forgive me, God, for ignoring you, for turning away from you. . . . Forgive me, God, for thinking that I could save myself, that if I just worked hard enough, or made enough money, or created what I thought was a stable home. . . . Forgive me for all of those false roads."

As I continued praying, long-submerged sins bubbled up to be confessed.

"God, forgive me, I had sex with a married man when I was in my twenties."

*Is that why my marriage went sour? Some cosmic "what goes around comes around"?*

Disturbed at the question, my eyes popped open and again took in the debris underfoot. I marveled that a "karma" idea could invade me in the midst of prayer and felt how easily my mind could be polluted. I had friends who believed we "manifest" everything that happens to us, and others who practiced a loose New Age "send energy into the universe" philosophy—all of it, a confusing jumble of human-directed fate, tangled around me like the weeds at my feet. It suddenly seemed fitting that Jesus watched over the garbage dump—the junk of humanity. I turned around and looked past the dumpsters to the coastline of Santa Monica and the ocean glinting in the sun.

*And there is God's beauty.*

As I walked home, relief came over me, perhaps from my pleas for forgiveness, which felt like coming clean, and perhaps from the acknowledgement of my weak and wandering mind, which felt like surrender.

It was similar to the sensation I'd felt when, at age thirty-five, I'd taken the first step in sobriety and "Admitted that we were powerless over alcohol and that our lives had become unmanageable." My prayers beside Jesus of the Garbage Dump revealed that I'd been powerless in my attempts to right my life and that my *mind* was unmanageable. Now, I felt the same restful relaxation that follows the surrender of futile self-direction.

I smiled, recalling the way I walked into my first AA meeting, back in New York. I literally wore a trench coat and sunglasses, still hiding. It wasn't until day three that I'd summoned the courage to raise my hand and say the words, "I'm Hattie and I'm an alcoholic." The relief was instant.

After the meeting, a lady came up to me and asked what I was going to do that afternoon.

"I don't know."

"Well, I think you should take a nap."

I looked at her skeptically.

"Think about it this way," she explained. "You've just found out that you have a fatal disease. Now, if you'd just learned you had cancer, what would you do? You'd take it easy. It's the same here. Eat something. Take a nap. Take it easy."

She told me to think of the word HALT, and make the letters stand for hungry, angry, lonely, and tired. She said we, who have this disease, should *never* let ourselves get too hungry, angry, lonely, or tired.

"Never let yourself be in HALT," she advised.

I laughed so hard I had to bend over.

"What is it? What's so funny?"

"I'm sorry. It's not you. It's just that . . . I've been in HALT my entire *life*."

"Oh, everyone thinks that."

"No, look at me," I gasped, finally overcoming my laughter. "Look into my eyes. I have been hungry, angry, lonely, and tired my entire life."

## Far from Home

I am not yet eighteen and I am in the Soviet Union, after several weeks in Berlin and London. John couldn't believe it when I left home this time.

"You mean, you're going abroad before I do?"

"This time you can say that," Lilly said. "Europe is abroad."

I am on another scholarship, and I haven't seen my family in more than a month. People here stare at me, with my long braids and Indian choker. The Russians seem to like American Indians.

Another college student offers me some hash. We smoke in the hotel room and look out at the Russians on the sidewalks, walking by in their grey clothes. Everyone wears grey here, so much so it feels like we got dropped into an old black and white movie.

It is 1972, and I wear tie dyed T-shirts and bell-bottom pants, causing Russians to turn and watch me walk by. Sometimes a guy will whisper "jeans." The other college students explain that they want to buy our jeans.

I miss home.

We study "comparative government." There are lectures in the morning, and in the afternoon tours to historical sites like cold art galleries and Lenin's dead body, encased in a glass tomb. We drink warm beer, and whenever possible smoke dope in the hotel room.

One day, when a guy whispers "jeans," I nod my head. He follows me, and waits outside my hotel while I change out of my jeans. Then with a jerk of his head and quick motions with his arms, he directs me to follow him. We walk several blocks until we get to a quiet street near the Moscow River, where he slips back into an entryway where we won't be seen. He hands me thirty rubles and I give him my jeans.

Scurrying back to the hotel, I hope thirty rubles is enough to call home.

"Hello?"

"Hi. It's me. It's Hattie."

The line crackles, making voices sound weak and tentative. Far away, the sisters take turns handing the receiver to one another to say hello, the way we used to do when Aunt Teddy called from

220

whatever missionary post she might be in. Reminded of her, I ask, "How's Aunt Teddy? Where is she now?"

"Oh, sorry, my turn's up, I have to get off. Here's John."

One by one, they hand me off. Because everyone is conscious of the high price of a long-distance call, and in the effort to make sure all get a chance to say "hi," every interchange is kept short. No conversation ever gets going and I forget to return to my question about Aunt Teddy.

It's not until a month later, when I'm back in the United States, that I learn Aunt Teddy is dead. She died of breast cancer while I was in the Soviet Union. Mom says she told everyone, "Shhh, don't tell Hattie," that day I called with my ruble money. Mom says she didn't want me to be sad, so far from home and all alone.

## Not Understanding

Mom was on my mind the day I did the Third Step. It was 1991 and I was about six months sober. The first two steps were easy enough: "Admit I am powerlessness over alcohol," and "Believe a power greater than myself could restore me to sanity." According to my sponsor, I didn't really have to determine what that "power" was.

"It could be the meetings themselves," she said. No need to take on the whole God question.

OK. But evasiveness ran out at Step Three. It was right there: "Make a decision to turn my life and will over to God, as I understand him." If you took Step Three, you made a decision. And you needed a God. The trouble was, I didn't know who that God might be.

John, who had done the steps of AA, was dead by then, so I couldn't ask him.

Mom was also gone, but I had an eagle feather that had been hers.

I turned it in my hand and held it up against the blue sky as I stood at the bottom of the Grand Canyon. I had flown from New York City, driven across the desert, and then ridden a pack mule eight miles down to the floor of the canyon to do my Third Step. Perhaps most people didn't go to such extremes. Maybe, for others, going to church or praying with their sponsor was all it took. But I didn't believe in church, and had complained when I learned that recovery meetings often end in the Lord's Prayer.

"Why this prayer? This is Christian. Why can't we pray something else?"

Just keep coming back, people told me.

Sometimes, the meetings ended with the Serenity Prayer, but even then I resisted.

"Why does it have to be 'God' who gives me the serenity? Why can't it be 'Goddess'?"

Just keep coming back, they said.

I didn't know who God was. I knew I was Native American and that we were supposed to believe in the powers of nature. Sometimes a wind rushing between the buildings of Manhattan would catch me in its gust, and I'd think, *There you are, God.*

If nature was God, then the Grand Canyon seemed a perfect cathedral for taking the Third Step. I chose the eagle feather for its spiritual symbolism to native peoples. *And because it was Mom's too*, I thought, as I hiked away from the campsite.

Alone, I scrambled up some red rocks at the bottom of a sheer cliff. It was shady and cool in the depths of the canyon, in stark contrast to the heat I'd endured on the ride down. Spotting a crevice in the rock, I stretched my arm toward it and planted the eagle feather in it.

"I turn my life and my will over to God," I said aloud, not understanding at all what I was doing.

# Chapter 30

"You have to forgive," said my friend.

I was getting Christian friends now. They were a new breed. They didn't feed revenge fantasies, or call down curses, or suggest shopping binges.

"I know," I grumbled.

It had seemed easy enough to enter into Christianity. All you had to do was accept a touch on the head. But to actually live as Jesus would have you live . . . that was not so easy.

That evening, I knelt and gave forgiveness a try.

"Dear God . . ."

But the words "I forgive" didn't form. My tongue wasn't co-operating. The best I could do was: "Dear God, please help me to forgive."

It was ten days until the deposition. The divorce wasn't final yet. My husband's lawyers had already tried to depose the doctor who'd discovered my cancer, and the family therapist I'd seen when I was weighing whether to try to save the marriage. A judge had refused to allow those depositions, and now, they wanted to depose *me*.

"Don't worry, I'll be right next to you," my lawyer said. "Get some rest."

Some rest? To me, the prescription could only be filled by a trip to my cabin.

Heart pounding, sweat forming on my forehead, I threw myself into clearing more lodgepole from the land. They grew so tightly together that the sun-starved trees died still standing upright. With a hand saw, I cut them and dragged them out of the forest in another effort to lessen the fire danger around the cabin. Blisters began to form on my fingers and my back ached as I lugged another thin, twenty-foot trunk from the woods.

In exhaustion, I sagged down onto the wooden steps of the cabin and gazed heavenward. Thin strings of cloud floated against the brilliant blue sky. I became mesmerized, discerning there were actually two layers of gauzy clouds, and only the lower layer was caught in a wind. As it glided below the higher layer, the lace of cloud made an ever-changing display. My soul lifted, and I understood the verse, "Be still and know that I am God."

That night, before I turned out the light in the loft, I opened the Bible and read:

> Let your conduct be without covetousness; be content with such things as you have. For He Himself has said, "I will never leave you nor forsake you." (Heb. 13:5 NKJV)

*Be content with such things as you have. What is God telling me? Settle this divorce? Don't ask for any wealth from his businesses and real estate?*

I turned out the light and stared into the blackness. My mind stirred. In the countdown to the deposition I'd gotten increasingly angry at what felt like injustice. I calculated the money he could earn in the future, and tossed and turned as I recounted the seventeen years that I'd been the higher earner in our home. It didn't seem fair that now, as his income was shooting up, I should walk away with nothing.

*Be content with such things as you have.*

The next morning, too tired to throw my body at the land, I climbed into my pickup truck to take a drive in the country. After two hours, I found myself in the tiny town of St. Ignatius, which seemed to hold little more than a church, a tavern, and a thrift store.

"That'll be two dollars," said the thrift store clerk.

I handed over the money and walked out with a Bible. I didn't need another one, but it was called a "Parallel Bible," with four translations for every word in it. And if that weren't enough, when I'd opened it in the store, I saw someone had written on the inside cover this notation: Isaiah 54. That was the Scripture Jeanie had told me to read last winter, the one that spoke to "a woman forsaken" (v. 6).

For thy Maker is thine husband. (v. 5 KJV)

Your Creator will be your "husband." (TLB)

For your Maker is your husband. (NKJV)

I carried the Bible to my truck, and carefully opened it. An index card fell out. On it, written in what looked like an old lady's hand, were these words: Matthew 5:25, Luke 12:58, Romans 12:20, Luke 6:27.

I flipped quickly to the first Scripture:

Settle matters quickly with your adversary who is taking you to court. Do it while you are still with him on the way. (Matt. 5:25)

I was so startled I snapped the book shut.

*OK, God. You could hardly be more clear.*

Last night I had read "be content with such things as you have," and this morning "settle matters quickly." The peaks of the Mission Mountains were vivid against the sky. I gazed in wonder at their clarity, feeling it as an exclamation mark to what I had just read. Slowly, I turned my eyes back to the book on my lap. It was no less majestic. I slid my hand over it, and paused before turning to the next Scripture noted on the index card, Luke 12:58.

> As you are going with your adversary to the magistrate, try hard to be reconciled to him.

I inhaled. The statement in Matthew was confirmed in Luke. I tried another translation.

> When thou goest with thine adversary to the magistrate, as thou art in the way, give diligence that thou mayest be delivered from him. (KJV)

My head fell back against the seat. I closed my eyes. "That thou mayest be delivered from him." *God is telling me to settle. I need to settle this divorce as quickly as possible.*

Turning to the third verse, I thought how improbable it was that some person had made these particular notations on an index card, and that the card was then forgotten in a Bible that was donated to a thrift store in a tiny town in Montana, that I happened to be in on that particular day, in my unique situation.

The next notation on the index card was Romans 12:20.

> Therefore if thine enemy hunger, feed him; if he thirst, give him drink. (KJV)

*I don't want to hear that. It's one thing to settle; it's another to "feed" him.*

As powerful as they were, I was disturbed by the messages: settle, get it done before you get to court, and if he's hungry, feed him. There was one last Scripture to look up. I hesitated before turning the pages, not sure that I wanted to hear what was so clearly being conveyed.

> But I tell you who hear me: Love your enemies, do good to those who hate you. (Luke 6:27)

*Loud and clear, God. Loud and clear.*

I carefully set the Bible and the index card on the passenger seat, started my truck, and drove back to the cabin. My world had changed again.

"Can we settle?" I asked my lawyer, when I got back to LA.

"We can't settle if we don't know what he's worth," she answered. "We subpoenaed his financial records way back in February. It's September and we still don't have the figures. How can we settle if we don't know how much he's worth?"

*But I don't care what he's worth. The Bible told me to settle.*

I knew that would sound insane.

"Can we make an offer?" I asked.

"An offer of what?" she returned. "It's impossible for our side to offer, or his side to offer, until we know what it is we're talking about."

*That depends on what the definition of "it" is*, I thought, remembering President Clinton's deposition.

Some days later, I turned on the car radio as I was driving home from work and discovered a call-in Christian radio show in progress. Someone was asking how to forgive when he didn't really want to do it, when it was anguish to even think of the person who had harmed him. I turned the radio up louder. The pastor, or host of the show, suggested the caller not try to force his heart to change but instead surrender his heart. "Give it to Jesus," he said.

*That sounds so cliché*, I thought, turning off the radio. I had hoped the host would have given the caller the exact words to use, words I could use. But at home, I attempted once again a forgiveness prayer.

"Jesus, as you would forgive, I ask you to help me forgive . . ."

To my surprise, forgiveness poured over my soon-to-be-ex-husband who was, after all, just another human being doing the best he could. The well of forgiveness was deep, and flowed far beyond him. Without intending to, I mumbled name after name, grudge after grudge, little and lots, old and young, recent and past. A torrent of hurt that I wasn't aware I was carrying streamed off me in tears that seemed to be running all on their own. It wasn't like normal crying. There were no sobs or hiccups, just water dripping from my closed eyes with each name and face that passed through my mind.

I forgave Mom and Dad their drinking.

I forgave the I Hate Hattie Club!

I forgave, and forgave . . .

Later, settling into bed, I thought about what a magnificent family I had. Mom and Dad, who loved each other and fought their way to the other side of awful, staying together until their deaths; my brother John, who used dancing and singing to distract us kids and grew up to become an actor and director; caretaker Lilly, who made the most of our scant resources, now working in economic development for our tribe; enterprising Annie, now grown-up Jo Ann running her own company, with offices on two coasts; irrepressible Carla, of dog-chasing and horse-wrangling fame, who helped our tribe reintroduce the wolf to Idaho and brought back Appaloosa horses to the reservation; high-flying Carlotta, fearlessly building wind towers; and Baby, the state senator.

I pulled the blankets up around me and wiped away more tears, thinking I could not have asked for better people to share my nest. But then I laughed, because "nest" brought to mind cuckoo-clock birds and runaway parakeets.

# Chapter 31

On the morning of the deposition, I woke determined to follow God's will, which meant I would agree to a settlement. But how that could come about I had no idea.

I showered, brushed my hair, put on makeup, and opened my closet.

*What does one wear to one's deposition?*

The ring of my cell phone made me jump.

"Hattie, read Psalm 55."

"OK," I said to my friend. It was the person I used to work with, the one who wore a cross and the one I had turned to back when I didn't know any other Christians.

> Listen to my prayer, O God,
>   do not ignore my plea;
>   hear me and answer me.
> My thoughts trouble me and I am distraught
>   at the voice of the enemy,
>   at the stares of the wicked;
> for they bring down suffering upon me
>   and revile me in their anger.

My heart is in anguish within me;
    the terrors of death assail me.
Fear and trembling have beset me;
    horror has overwhelmed me.
I said, "Oh, that I had the wings of a dove!
    I would fly away and be at rest—
I would flee far away
    and stay in the desert; [Selah]
I would hurry to my place of shelter,
    far from the tempest and storm."

Confuse the wicked, O Lord, confound their speech,
    for I see violence and strife in the city.
Day and night they prowl about on its walls;
    malice and abuse are within it.
Destructive forces are at work in the city;
    threats and lies never leave its streets.

If an enemy were insulting me,
    I could endure it;
if a foe were raising himself against me,
    I could hide from him.
But it is you, a man like myself,
    my companion, my close friend,
with whom I once enjoyed sweet fellowship
    as we walked with the throng at the house of God.

Let death take my enemies by surprise;
    let them go down alive to the grave,
    for evil finds lodging among them.

But I call to God,
    and the LORD saves me.
Evening, morning and noon
    I cry out in distress,
    and he hears my voice.

He ransoms me unharmed
   from the battle waged against me,
    even though many oppose me.
God, who is enthroned forever,
   will hear them and afflict them— [Selah]
men who never change their ways
   and have no fear of God.

My companion attacks his friends;
   he violates his covenant.
His speech is smooth as butter,
   yet war is in his heart;
his words are more soothing than oil,
   yet they are drawn swords.

Cast your cares on the Lord
   and he will sustain you;
   he will never let the righteous fall.
But you, O God, will bring down the wicked
   into the pit of corruption;
bloodthirsty and deceitful men
   will not live out half their days.

But as for me, I trust in you. (Ps. 55)

As I read it again, certain phrases took shape. "If an enemy were insulting me . . . if a foe raised himself against me . . . but it is you . . . my close friend, with whom I once enjoyed sweet fellowship." My husband. "My companion . . . violates his covenant." He had hired three high-powered law firms in Los Angeles and New York. And they were about to depose me.

I stood and reached for whatever was nearest in the closet, no longer caring what I wore. The final message of the Psalm buoyed me: *The Lord saves me. "He ransoms me unharmed from the battle waged against me, even though many oppose me"* (v. 18).

Not knowing how the Lord might ransom me, but confident of his care, I drove to the deposition more calm than I could ever have predicted I'd be.

The room fell silent as I entered. His lawyers were lined up along the opposite side of the conference table, with their backs to the window. He sat in the farthest corner looking down at his long, thin fingers. A court reporter and camera operator were set up at the right. No one said, "Good morning."

My attorneys slid into chairs on our side of the table. I was the last to sit. There appeared to be a concerted effort on everyone's part to avoid eye contact. It was so ludicrously silent that each throat cleared or paper shuffled seemed to jar the air.

## Think about It

"Thou preparest a table before me," says Teddy.

"Thou preparest a table before me," I repeat, looking up into her blue-grey eyes.

"In the presence of mine enemies."

"How come?" I ask. "Why do I have to have a table in the presence of my enemies?"

We are walking in the backyard of the Beacon Hill house, careful not to step in Shadow's poop. Teddy takes a seat on the back porch step and I stand before her.

"Well, think about it," she says. "Listen to the words once more: 'Thou *preparest* a table before me.' That means God is setting up a table for you, probably filled with food and good things."

"I get that, but why are my enemies there?" I ask, taking her hands in mine.

"It means, *even* if your enemies are there, God is going to take care of you. He prepares a table for you right in front of your enemies. They can't stop him from taking care of you."

232

"Oh. How does it go again?"

"Thou preparest a table before me, in the presence of mine enemies."

## Resting in God

The deposition was scheduled to last all day, and possibly into the next, but before noon those on the opposite side of the table offered a settlement: ownership of the house in exchange for releasing all other claims.

"I'll take it," I told my lawyer, as we huddled in a side room, away from the conference table.

"What about the building in Beverly Hills?" she asked.

"I don't want it."

"What about the condo in Hawaii?"

"I don't want anything connected with him."

*"Settle matters quickly with your adversary who is taking you to court."*

"What about alimony, should you lose your job in the future?"

I shook my head.

"You were married seventeen years. You're entitled to alimony."

No thanks. The Lord will provide.

I was free. Resting in God meant I didn't have to scratch for every bit that might be due me. It was a revolution. The literal hunger for food that I had experienced in childhood had created in me a hypervigilance for sustenance and safety. It probably propelled me throughout my career to do more, work harder, make sure I had every base covered. And yet, it was with utmost peace that I agreed not to seek future provision from the person across the table. I didn't need it. The real provision was now inside me.

I have been crucified with Christ; it is no longer I who live, but Christ lives in me; and the life which I now live in the flesh I live by

233

faith in the Son of God, who loved me and gave Himself for me. (Gal. 2:20 NKJV)

Weeks later, I stood on the shore, curling my bare toes in the sand.

The setting sun cast an orange glow on the Pacific and on the seventy people gathered on the beach. A young man played guitar and some in the crowd sang hymns as our pastor waded into the waves.

Within the group of spectators I had my own support team: one who'd given me refuge during the year, a few from my Bible study, and my good friend whom I'd once thought of as "the Christian at work."

The sun approached its reflection, bathing the crowd in its brilliance. The pastor called out, "There's no particular order. Just come on in when you're ready."

My body sprang forward, my feet flying over the sand. I was the first to splash into the sea for my baptism, eager for my new life.

❖ ❖ ❖ ❖

"And the last verse. Ready for this one?" Teddy asks, brushing some bangs out of my eyes.

"Yep."

"OK, repeat after me," she says, slipping her hand to my chin and gently turning my face to hers.

"Surely goodness and mercy shall follow me . . ."

"Surely goodness and mercy shall follow me . . ."

"All the days of my life." She smiles.

"All the days of my life." I grin back at her.

"And I shall dwell in the house of the Lord, forever."

"And I shall dwell in the house of the Lord . . . forever."

# Epilogue

*It should be somewhere in this lower section,* I thought, heading down the slope toward a grove of cedar trees.

Trying not to step on any graves, I left a trail of footprints in the wet grass that zigzagged at sharp angles past and between horizontal headstones. I stopped to study the map once more, attempting to reconcile the crosshatches on the piece of paper the cemetery office had given me with the name plates spread out at my feet.

"These are the two hundreds . . . The Kauffmans are supposed to be in this section," I muttered to myself.

The cemetery, north of Seattle, had ground-level plates marking each spot. With no upright tombstones, the place looked like a vast and peaceful park blanketed in every shade of green. It was so verdant that even the metal name markers were edged in greenish moss. There was no stopping life here.

I was searching for Aunt Teddy's burial place.

*It must be this way,* I figured, and began descending the slope. As a teenager I had never asked to see her grave. Nor had I looked for it when I lived in Seattle during my twenties. But last night, I'd flown up from Los Angeles to find it. And now, four decades after her death, I came upon the grave marker.

*Theodora Kauffman, November 5, 1928–August 11, 1972*

"So young," I whispered, "younger than me." I squatted down to trace my fingers over the raised lettering. "Theodora."

Theo *means God, and* Dora *means gift. Her name meant "gift of God."*

I smiled. And the physical act of smiling made me aware that my emotions were not what I'd expected them to be. Perhaps I'd thought the grave would be a place I could tell Teddy that I was sorry . . . sorry I hadn't been there when she died, sorry I had rejected her so meanly. But sorrowful regret wasn't in this quiet moment at her graveside. Instead, I felt almost like giggling at the big billboard of her name hidden behind the simple "Teddy."

I turned my head to the sky.

Thank you . . . for the gift. Thank you.

To learn more about

# Hattie Kauffman

or to book her to speak at your next event,
visit www.hattiekauffman.com.

Fans of Hattie Kauffman